To my f..

Getting to Know You

LETTERS TO MY FAMILY

by
Eleanor King Byers

— and bridge buddy —

Fondly,

Eleanor

FriesenPress

One Printers Way
Altona, MB R0G 0B0
Canada

www.friesenpress.com

Copyright © 2023 by Eleanor King Byers
First Edition — 2023

All rights reserved.

No part of this publication may be reproduced in any form, or by any means, electronic or mechanical, including photocopying, recording, or any information browsing, storage, or retrieval system, without permission in writing from FriesenPress.

ISBN
978-1-03-918760-3 (Hardcover)
978-1-03-918759-7 (Paperback)
978-1-03-918761-0 (eBook)

1. BIOGRAPHY & AUTOBIOGRAPHY, PERSONAL MEMOIRS

Distributed to the trade by The Ingram Book Company

For my children, Diane and Stephen, and my grandchildren, Brendan, Andrew, Lindsay, and Kalyn …

… so you will get to know your forebears.

Table of Contents

—Introduction—
1

—Chapter One—

Grandparents
3

—Chapter Two—

Great War Heroes
35

—Chapter Three—

Civilian Heroes
81

—Chapter Four—

Parents
131

—Chapter Five—

Brother Don
191

—Afterword—
251

Acknowledgements
255

"You have to go back to your roots to see what it is that drives you, and what it is that makes you who you are."

Singer/songwriter/actor Sting

—Introduction—

Actually, this story began twenty years ago when I wrote my first book, a memoir entitled, *The House With The Light On*, in which I wrote of my years growing up in Calgary in the '40s and '50s, inarguably the best time and place to be a kid. My tale revolved around my beloved family, but I always regretted that I did not have more words for my grandparents. The simple truth is, I did not know them; I had entered this world after all my grandparents had departed from it. Well, that's not entirely true … I did have my maternal grandfather for eight days, but that scarcely counted. Eight days didn't even allow us a nuzzle.

Then a few years ago, I read an article addressing the supposition that a good many of our inherited characteristics skip a generation, the author suggesting that we have a greater likelihood of acquiring attributes and mannerisms from our grandparents than from our parents. This theory was especially intriguing to me, having known these important family members only vicariously through tales told to me by my parents and my aunts and uncles. Now I longed to know them better.

When my parents died, I became the beneficiary of the family's famous boxes—the repositories for our memorabilia—letters, journals, photos, coins, collectibles of every description. The boxes had been part of our household my whole life, so, unthinkingly, I had assigned them to a corner of our basement, where they began collecting new layers of dust on top of the old. But now, their time had come; I would raise them from the dead to launch my getting-to know-my-grandparents quest.

Beyond the boxes, I had also journeyed to the birth sites of each grandparent, and paid each one a visit at their gravesites as well. Yet when all was said and done, one truth was undeniable: the artefacts that rose to the top—that consistently set my heart aflutter—were family letters. Then one day it dawned on me—*finally*—that's it! Letters! What took you so long? Letters are the path to knowing your grandparents. And so, I began, "Dear Grandpa …" And Grandpa replied.

The mere act of writing to my grandparents magically brought them to life. Every chat through a letter was pure joy. Eventually, the magical journey led me to the family members that I had known—my parents and aunts and uncles. I could bring them back with letters, too. Think of all the things I never got around to saying … or asking! Soon, I was understanding them better and appreciating them more.

Then my bachelor brother, now ailing, returned to Calgary after an absence of more than fifty years. Don was the member of the family closest to me in age, and the one I knew best. At least I thought I did. When he died, he left behind *his* boxes—nineteen of them—packed to the hilt! As I sifted through his profusion of paper—mainly letters and manuscripts—I felt my familiar bro at my side … that is until a stranger popped up on the occasional page. Never mind, there was a solution. Write him, too.

And so, I wrote them all. And I left no words unsaid.

—Chapter One—
Grandparents

Paternal Grandfather
Henry Clement King

Born May 31, 1869—Preston, Lancashire, England
Died November 29, 1924—Birmingham, West Midlands, England

Dear Grandpa,

You must have been like a fish out of water. Imagine loving musical theatre as much as you did, and being born into a British cotton mill town. Here's what I know about your beginnings: You were the second-born of seven children to Henry King and Elizabeth Wignall King. You had five sisters and just one brother. Your father, a redhead, originally hailed from Barrowford, a village east of Preston. He worked as a spinner and weaver alongside many of the area's native sons in one of Preston's famed cotton mills. Then one day the local jewellery store came up for sale, and impulsively he bought it—why not?—it would provide a far more attractive way of life than the monotony of the mill. It called for him to learn the delicate task of watch repair, which I assume he mastered somehow. Your family lived conveniently above the jewellery store, and faithfully attended the Methodist Church every Sunday morning. I understand your father was also a skilled flautist. It's been suggested that traits tend to skip a generation, but from what I see, your father's love for music—and his red hair—have made an appearance in *every* generation succeeding his.

When you were very young, you followed in the footsteps of your father, entering the jewellery business and apprenticing as a watchmaker. Eventually, you struck out on your own, venturing into the high-rent district in the centre of Preston to establish your own enterprise. Your new jewellery store promoted *H.C. King's Lucky Wedding Rings*. I find the catchphrase amusing, knowing that my father would have taken issue with *luck* having any bearing on the success of a marriage. What I want to know, Grandpa, is whether you think that labelling wedding rings *lucky* actually boosted sales. I hope so; your inventive catchphrase does have a ring to it! (Forgive the pun, but I am a product of my *punning* dad.) I understand that, before long, however, you weren't entirely wrapped up in rings. Your keen love of music had progressed from a passing fancy to a persistent distraction. In the absence of any other explanation, I have to assume that music was the driving force behind your next move.

You left the Methodist church of your upbringing to join the church of its origins, the Church of England, where you were officially baptized and confirmed. Family tales suggest the drawing card of this church was its fine parish choir, which offered an opportunity for your bass baritone voice. But there was a bonus, wasn't there? I'm guessing the engaging young songbird in the contralto section of the choir caught your eye the first day. And from descriptions I have of you—a man of action—I suspect that you wasted no time in making your next move. I picture you sweeping Grandma right off her feet, popping one of your lucky rings on her finger before she even had a chance to say yes … or no. Of course, you would not have taken no for an answer in any event. And so you were married in the Church of England in Preston, on February 18, 1891. You were just twenty-one years old, and Grandma one year older.

You and Grandma produced seven children, although my generation would think of the Kings as a family of five, because you tragically lost your first two in infancy early on. We only knew them through family stories. But that doesn't mean that I haven't given a lot of thought to your unimaginable loss. I remember Dad telling me a heart-wrenching story of Frank, your firstborn, dying at only six months of age, a story that you must have told him at some time. Frank was a healthy, robust child, and the apple of your eye. You left for work one morning, striding the front walkway with a whistle in your step, as always, and turned to wave goodbye to your beautiful little boy, gurgling in the living room window, where Grandma was proudly holding him up. After you disappeared from their view, she put him in his crib for his morning nap ... and he never woke up. How do you carry on after such a crushing blow? If the story was remembered accurately, Frank's death might be diagnosed today as SIDS—Sudden Infant Death Syndrome—a frightful anomaly that snatches children, like a thief, in their sleep.

Then, before you scarcely had time to recover from that loss, your second child, a precious little girl, Madge, was taken from you at just three months old. My cousin Ethel has recorded her death as "intestinal blockage." However, I recall my Aunt Millie suggesting that Madge died from a smallpox vaccination, which is another thing entirely. Interesting how conflicting stories come to us, isn't it? I will say that vaccination merits consideration since this period marked the dawn of immunization, when vaccine contamination was regrettably all too common. You will know the correct story, of course, but regardless of the cause, the pain is still crushing, and it never goes away.

And so, the family of five that became part of our lives were Arthur, Walter, Mildred, Henry Clement (Harry), and Horace, my father. Four sons was quite a departure from all those sisters you had. This might be as good a time as any to comment on your choice of Christian names for our famous five. To tell you the truth, I've always been a bit puzzled that four of them were given only one name, while you bestowed Uncle Harry, your fourth child, with two—specifically your own given names. It seems to me the others were shortchanged. Just saying. I don't know that it mattered to any of them, and I don't recall Uncle Harry lording it over the rest of them, but then there's a lot I don't know. While I'm on names, I have to tell you a funny story. Whenever I thought of your name—I mean other than Grandpa—I thought of you as Henry. Yet for reasons I could never explain, the name Clem floated about in the recesses of my mind. Then one day not so long ago, I came across an envelope amongst my mother's effects containing a mishmash of collectibles. On a small envelope inside the bigger one, Mother had written "Grandpa King" and below that in brackets ("Clem"). There you go. You were Clem all along. So now I've said goodbye to Henry. There was nothing inside that small envelope, by the way, but finding Clem on the outside was a windfall.

Back in 1985, my husband, Dick, and I made a special trek to your hometown of Preston, where we looked up landmarks—Dad's birthplace on Bence Road, the family home on Manchester Road, the family's parish church, *Lingards Menswear*, where Uncle Harry worked, and the address on Fishergate Street where your jewellery store was once located. *Lingards* was still operating as quite a tony menswear store, while your jewellery store had become *Wakefields Stores*, a far-from-tony ladies-wear store. Filling its two large windows were enormous yellow SALE signs, looking suspiciously like they resided there permanently. Promise you won't laugh at me when I tell you about one place on my list that we had trouble finding—Aynem Park—a favourite place of Dad's, which he talked about endlessly. Apparently, bikes were forbidden in the park, but that didn't stop him from regularly riding his bike from one end of the park to the other, frequently with a breathless bobby in pursuit on foot. Poor bobby never stood a chance. (You're probably not supposed to know this.) Dad described the location of the park as being very near the family home, so Dick and I circled and circled the area, but for the life of us we could not find Aynem Park. I'm embarrassed to tell you how many times we passed Avenham Park before I figured it out! It's all in the pronunciation.

After returning home from that trip, I began delving into Preston's history out of curiosity, and, wow, did I stumble on an intriguing story. It's compelling enough that I'm sure my dad would have told it to us had he known about it, so I'm assuming he didn't. It goes like this: A Preston native son by the name of Joseph Livesey, on noting that drinking and fighting were becoming an everyday way of life for the men working in the mills, wrote to the press about his concern with spreading drunkenness in the town. After his words reached the people, he courageously took the next step: he announced a personal pledge of total abstinence, and urged others to join him. In 1832, seven Preston men, including Livesey, formally signed a pledge to abstain from alcohol. One of the seven, Richard "Dicky" Turner, an illiterate fish hawker—and known drunkard—became an early, faithful convert. When someone suggested to Dicky that abstinence only meant *spirits* and that beer and wine were acceptable, Dicky's reply was unequivocal: "Nothing but the tee-total will do." Some adherents suggested that Dicky, known to stutter, stumbled over the word t-t-total; others believed that he emphasized the letter "t" to highlight the word total, which he strongly advocated. In any event, the word "teetotal" stuck and is still recognized the world over today. But there's more to the story.

Apparently, 2,000 men made a commitment immediately following the signing by the Preston seven, and, within two years, 28,000 had signed the pledge. Temperance societies sprang up all over Lancashire and beyond. Well, Grandpa, this all took place long before your time, but I think you would have applauded the idea, and taken pride in the example set by your hometown. I do know that alcohol never played a role in the life of your offspring, and that we kids were the happy beneficiaries of their raucous, zany antics performed cold sober. To this day, I don't know if my teetotaling father ever knew that the moniker was coined in his hometown. So, that's my story of Preston. Now let's get back to yours.

I know that while keeping the wolf from the door with your jewellery business, you were satisfying your hunger for music by sidelining in light opera. The family spoke of your roles in Gilbert and Sullivan's *The Mikado* and *The Gondoliers*, and especially of a coveted role as Harry Sherwood in *Dorothy*. Eventually, you added choirmaster for your church to your résumé, while taking on another couple of choirs on the side. And I have evidence that you were a tough taskmaster, which was doubtless necessary to maintain order on your crowded calendar. I have a postcard, embellished with your rendering of a policeman, addressed in your handwriting to a member of one of your choirs. It reads: "Dear Sir/. The first rehearsal of the Policeman's Chorus will take place at the above address on Friday night—at 7:30 prompt—your attendance will oblige. Yours truly, H. C. King." It boggles my mind how you'd organize a policeman's choir practice without the expedience of email or at the very least a telephone. (I'll try to explain what email is another time.)

In spite of this very full life you'd carved out for yourself, you were clearly restless for something bigger, and you'd decided that you were not going to find it in Preston. So you set your sights on Canada, a much-loved Commonwealth sister, a young land of opportunity. I have

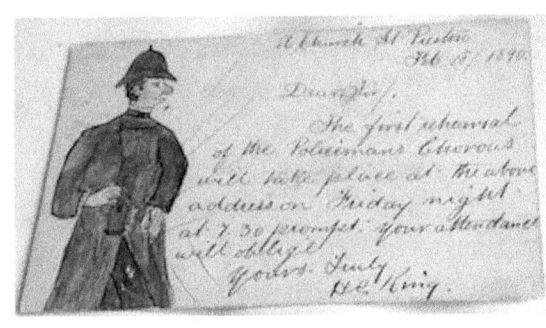

so many questions I want to ask you about this venture, Grandpa. Did you plan for this move over a period of years, or did you just get up one day and decide you were going? One minute I think you must have saved up for a long time to prepare for such a move, then the next I think you weren't the kind of guy who had that kind of patience. You'd just sell your material goods, pack the proceeds—and your bank account—in your wallet, and off you'd go. It would all work out. Where there's a will …

So I don't know the preamble to this venture, but I do know some particulars: You set sail on the *S. S. Canada* from Liverpool on June 15, 1905, landing at Quebec City on June 27. From there, you travelled to the Toronto area, where you spent the next month exploring possibilities. You chose Grenfell, Saskatchewan. Which begs the question, what drew you there? Was there a jewellery business for sale? Had Grenfell sent out an appeal for a timekeeper for the railway? A call for a church choir leader? I know you would have qualified for all of the above, but there's so many fragments of your early years in Canada that end in a question mark. In any event, on August second you boarded a train heading west carrying all your worldly goods, and disembarked at Grenfell.

That first brutal Saskatchewan winter must have tested the family's mettle, but evidently you passed the test, because you stayed for five years. My dad was too young to retain any memories of the Grenfell years, but Aunt Millie spoke frequently of the town, always highlighting her fondness for Penepekish, the little Indian girl who lived on the reservation adjacent to your home. Penepekish became her best friend, a welcome circumstance after weeks and months of brothers-only company.

The most repeated stories Aunt Millie told of the Grenfell years surrounded your love for musical theatre—namely, the production of plays in which you took lead roles that showcased your wonderful voice. However, Aunt Millie also hinted that there was a downside to your musical involvements—they were running interference with the jewellery business, the family's main source of income. Grandma's focus was feeding her flock, so she began agitating for you to spend more time *minding the shop*. The problem now was that you were so heavily involved with your musical affairs in this small town that extricating yourself had become near impossible. And so you agreed to move, with an assurance that you'd buckle down to business in a new town. A fresh start with a clean slate.

On May 24, 1910, the family packed up and moved farther west to Wainwright, Alberta, a town of 400 people, arriving the very year that it was incorporated as a town. I can see eyes rolling in the church that first Sunday, when the exuberant King family filed in and filled an entire pew. When the opening hymn began, heads swivelled at the sound of the bass baritone booming forth from that pew. And of course, the minister just happened to be in dire need of a choirmaster, so he pounced on you immediately after the service. Grandpa, you rascal. So much for the clean slate! Grandma knew the gig was up; you were back in the thick of it before you'd even hung the shingle on your new jewellery store.

Aunt Millie used to describe that Sunday scene this way: "Mother threw up her arms in despair, but underneath she was proud as punch of Dad and his musical talents." And so, Grandma gave in to your need for music and theatre in your life, and rolled up her sleeves to pitch in wherever you needed her—in the home, in the jewellery store or assisting with the theatrical productions. In fact, she became chief costume designer and seamstress for the many plays you wrote and produced. The two of you were clearly the first couple of theatre in Wainwright. But you didn't stop there.

Dad used to describe Wainwright as *the liveliest town in Alberta*, while offering much of the credit to you. He said you left your mark on just about every aspect of the town. You weren't satisfied with just running a jewellery store, or accepting the role as choirmaster for the church, or writing and directing plays. You added two further items to your résumé: you became the town reeve and the watch inspector for the Grand Trunk Railway. Yet in spite of all those involvements, the thing that my dad was most proud of was the part you played in establishing the Buffalo Park. As a seven-year-old, he thrilled at the spectacle of fifteen carloads of buffalo, imported from Montana, arriving at the local train station. The tumult of 190 buffalo clunking down ramps in a cloud of dust was imprinted on his brain forever.

Finally, I'll let you in on a secret: one day when I was visiting my dad when he was in his eighties and requiring the assistance of a long-term care facility, he began reminiscing about you and your love of theatre. "Deep down," he said, "I fully believe that my father had the potential to make a successful full-time career of it." My heart skipped a beat. How many gifted people missed their chance because of outside circumstances? I used to think that Dad, himself, belonged in theatre. If it's any consolation, Grandpa, you've left your mark with all your grandchildren in any event. In spite of the fact that none of us knew you, we've all gone through life carrying the same vision—we see you in full costume on the stage.

Well, Grandpa, I'm guessing the Kings would have continued to live happy, productive lives in Wainwright indefinitely, had a war not broken out in Europe. Patriots that you were, you answered the call to serve. I'll write again soon, and maybe we can travel through the war years together. Till then, keep singing!

Love,
Your granddaughter,
Eleanor

Paternal Grandmother
Florence Kate Potter King

Born October 17, 1868—Preston, Lancashire, England
Died June 19, 1928—Calgary, Alberta, Canada

Dear Grandma,

I have a huge desire to know you, but so far, you're a bit of an enigma. I struggle to get a feel for your personality. I hope that will change as I write. If I were to rely on photos for help, I have only three of you—two that include family members, and the third, a head-and-shoulders solitary. I believe the family photos were a requirement for passport applications, when immigrating to Canada initially, and then a second time. You look a bit stern in the earlier one taken in 1905. Actually, I might better describe your look as beleaguered. But is it any wonder? You're about to set sail across the Atlantic Ocean with five young children and no assurances for how you're going to survive on the other side. You're leaving behind your large, supportive Potter family, those who knew you best and loved you unconditionally.

This particular photo, the only one in existence of the seven of you assembled, tells a whole story. My dad, your baby, is wedged between you and Grandpa seated on a bench, and if I examine it closely, it looks to me like you might have the little imp's arm in a concealed vice grip, out of necessity, to facilitate the photographer. Grandpa looks as happy as a guy can look when he's not allowed to smile, but sure wants to. Arthur, standing in back, displays an air of calm and patience, traits of the responsible oldest child. Millie, standing to your left, has a look of wonder mixed with signs of long-suffering, typical of a girl beset with four brothers. Cross-legged on the floor in front sit Harry, looking like he'd like to get the show on the road, and Walter, cocky and defiant, ready to take on whatever comes.

The solo photo of you tells a whole other story: you are sophisticated and lovely in a black fur coat, elegant cloche hat, and wire-rimmed glasses. You're a little older in this photo, and you're revealing a hint of a smile, which emits warmth. I smile back at you, thinking you've probably reached that stage in life where the children have become independent and you finally have time for yourself.

Beyond the photos, I essentially know you only through stories that Dad and Aunt Millie occasionally related. And of course a daughter's memory of her mother will differ from a son's. I picture you leaning on your only daughter to share the burden of the housework out of sheer necessity. Keeping your five men fed and in clean clothes would have been a mammoth job. I never asked Aunt Millie whether her dad or brothers ever pitched in with the cooking or the laundry, or if they viewed it as "woman's work." I only know that she adored her brothers and never complained that they didn't carry their share of the load. But then, she never complained about anything. That was just her. As far as Dad was concerned I do know that he loved you dearly, and I've never forgotten what he once said to me: "Any good that I've become is thanks to my mother." That speaks volumes, Grandma, knowing the world of good that was my dad.

You'll be pleased to know that my cousin Ethel did some genealogy research of the King and Potter family trees, which has offered us at least a glimpse of your beginnings. You were the eighth of nine children—five girls and four boys—born to William Ely Potter and Rhoda Holbrook Potter, in Preston, Lancashire. When I look up Preston on a map, I can see that it sits halfway between Glasgow and London. Your father worked for the Stephen Simpson firm, gold thread embroidery specialists, a business that evidently held quite a place of honour in the city's history. I'm told that their most notable assignment was the embroidery work on the uniforms for the staff of the magnificent, though ill-fated ship, Titanic. The embroidery plant outlived the Titanic, operating for a record 180 years before it succumbed to Preston's redevelopment in 2009.

I'm saddened to learn that your mother died when you were only nine years old. I can't begin to imagine such a loss. Your little sister Julia, just four years old, was placed in the hands of your father's brother Charles and his wife Rhoda, who raised her as their only child. Here come the questions: Did Julia know the circumstances of her adoption? Was she raised to understand that all these older "cousins" were, in fact, her siblings? I'm sure she was well loved, regardless. When I examine the family tree, I see that four of your siblings (Julia included) remained childless, while the other five of you produced twenty-seven children amongst you. You and Grandpa certainly did your fair share. But I'm getting ahead of myself.

The story goes that as a young woman you sang in your parish choir, and one day a booming bass voice joined the choir. Life can turn on a dime, can't it? Family lore has always suggested that Grandpa heard your sweet voice rise from the contralto section, and that was it, he'd found the one for him. That story has romantic appeal, but I'll be honest, I have trouble believing that he heard anything above his own thunderous voice. In any event, you found each other, and you made beautiful music together.

You supported one another through the unimaginable heartache of losing your first two children in infancy, and went on to produce the wonderful family that filled my world. Descriptions of Grandpa suggest that he was a take-charge kind of guy, so I've always wondered whether you and he spent long hours discussing the idea of moving to Canada, or whether he just arrived home from work one night, and said, "Pack our bags, Florence, the boat sails tomorrow." I've never known whether you were a willing participant or not. In any event, you packed, and off you went. Arthur, the eldest was only ten years old when you set sail for Canada, and my dad, the youngest was a toddler of two and a half. You must have questioned the sanity of this major undertaking the very first day aboard ship when you encountered rough seas, and everyone came down with a nightmarish case of sea sickness ... everyone, that is, except the littlest guy, who escaped it entirely. To his great delight, little Horace had the run of the ship for twelve days because no one had the strength or the will to ride herd on him. When I reflect on this unbridled freedom that my father enjoyed at such a tender age, I wonder if it didn't become his assumption for life.

After that rough Atlantic crossing, you made your way to Grenfell, Saskatchewan, and a prairie winter that must have been another attack on your system. By all accounts, it was the local church that came to your rescue—a godsend indeed—embracing you and your family. It was also Grandpa's launching pad for his musical productions, which he loved so much. Except I understand they took a lot of time away from the jewellery business, your bread and butter. Amateur theatre doesn't pay the bills, does it? So after five years, you both agreed to a fresh start.

The gang boarded the train once again, and chugged farther west to Wainwright, Alberta. My dad was old enough to remember the Wainwright years, and he did so with great fondness. Forgive me for chuckling at reports that your new beginnings failed to bring about the intended changes; I understand Grandpa was very soon off and running again, and this time, not only his beloved musical pursuits, but pretty much everything else in town. So, Grandma, you must have eventually said to yourself, "If you can't beat 'em, join 'em." I do know that you rolled up your sleeves and became Grandpa's first mate, designing and sewing all the costumes for his theatrical productions. And if that wasn't enough, you made your way into the kitchen to cook for the hungry hordes at the post-concert dinners and dances.

You carried an unimaginable workload, yet I have a feeling that you'd now be willing to admit that the Wainwright years were some of your best, a time when the whole family joined forces to support Grandpa's endeavours. The Elite Theatre in Wainwright was kept hopping with the King family productions. Every member of the family stepped up to sing, dance, play piano, play flute, recite poetry, or engage in a combination of the above for the annual *Thanksgiving Dinner and Concert* or the *Great Patriotic Banquet, Concert and Dance*—always dressed to the nines in the grand stage wear that you created. Aunt Millie must've felt like a princess in the flouncy dress you made for her solo presentations, and Hollywood would have envied Uncle Harry's *Robin Hood*. I wish I had a picture of my dad's attire for his performance in *Dick Whittington and His Cat*. He was very proud of his role as the cat. Did you know that Aunt Millie preserved many of your fabulous costumes in her trunk for years? What a heyday we had as kids, digging through her treasure trove for Halloween costumes.

With all this excitement filling your life, you were also proudly watching four fine young sons grow into manhood, and a darling daughter develop into a capable young woman. I think you may have coasted along in Wainwright forever had a war not loomed overseas. Let's save that story for next time.

Love you, Grandma!
Your granddaughter, Eleanor

P.S. I can't help thinking of my other grandmother as I write. I'm pretty sure the two of you never met. Grandmother Anderson was five years older than you, but she didn't start her family until after you had finished yours. Between the ages of twenty-four and thirty-four, you gave birth to seven children. Grandmother Anderson married late and had only two children: her first—my mother—at age thirty-nine and her second—my Aunt Lil—at age forty-three. The two of you came from widely dissimilar backgrounds, yet you had much in common: you both lost a parent when you were only nine years old; you both became isolated from your extended families early in your marriages; you both raised your children early in the twentieth century; you both drew vital support from your churches; you both prevailed under modest—if not meagre—means; you both contributed to the welfare of your households as skilled seamstresses. And you both died far too young: you were just shy of your sixtieth birthday, and Grandmother Anderson died two days after turning sixty-one.

Maternal Grandfather
Reuben Robinson Anderson

Born August 20, 1860—Aultsville, Ontario, Canada
Died September 30, 1937—Calgary, Alberta, Canada

Dear Grandpa,

You have a special place in my heart, because you were the only living grandparent I ever had. Except I only had you for eight days, time enough for you to hold me in your heart even though you were never given an opportunity to cradle me in your arms. My dad used to tell the story of running the news of my birth from Mother's bedside in the hospital, where she was confined, to your bedside in the extended care hospital a few blocks away, where you lay terminally ill. It was the middle of the night, but that wasn't going to stop my dad from delivering the good news. He was beside himself with excitement as he snuck past the nurses' station and tiptoed into your room with his big surprise. But the surprise was on him: you sat upright in bed and announced jubilantly, "It's a girl!" Dad's only explanation for this turn of events was that an angel must have slipped into your room in the night, beating him to the draw with the news. I rather like his idea of an angel announcing my arrival, don't you? Do you think our angel has been sending messages between us ever since?

But enough of my entrance into the world, let's go back to yours, whether it was heralded by an angel or not. You were the fourth of eight children born to Francis Anderson, a carriage-maker, and Ann Loan Anderson, in Aultsville, Ontario, in 1860. I'm sure you could tell me many stories about your childhood in Aultsville, but I would have to write the closing chapter; you'd never imagine what happened to your hometown. A massive seaway project was developed in 1954 to expand the St. Lawrence River, in order to facilitate large transportation ships through to the Great Lakes. The project could only meet its goal by submerging the villages and surrounding habitat that stood in its path. I hate to tell you this, but Aultsville is actually now under water, remembered only as one of the ten *Lost Villages of Ontario*.

During the first step of the project, enormous machines clawed their way through your hometown and the surrounding villages, plowing under trees, roads, buildings, leaving nothing but wasteland in their wake. Then, in the resulting barren expanse, canals, locks, and dams were built, until the depth of the waterway increased from fourteen to twenty-seven feet.

A few select historic homes and buildings were spared and moved into newly established towns on higher ground. Graves, as you might expect, were a major issue, and took special planning. In most cases—all the Anderson graves, I understand—the gravesites themselves were loaded down with rocks before the flooding, and only the gravestones were moved upland to a cemetery established solely to accommodate them. I can scarcely comprehend such a project. To the locals, displaced by the thousands, the whole affair must have felt like a holocaust.

I have read accounts of former residents who expressed great sorrow when watching helplessly as their homes were crushed before their eyes. One woman, who was a child at the time, described the wrenching sight of her father slumped on their back stoop, head in hands, crying uncontrollably as his whole way of life was being ripped out from under him. Another remembered her mother's response to the family home being spared for moving: ignoring the command to vacate before moving day, she remained firmly planted in her rocking chair in the middle of the living room as her beloved home was dislodged from its moorings. She resolutely rocked all the way up to Ingleside, her assigned new town.

I'm not sure if I should tell you the story of your original family home, but I guess you're already prepared for news that it's gone. For what it's worth, it was evidently the last one in town to go under. My second cousin Nick (grandson of Clayton) heard the story firsthand from a woman who had grown up in the house, her father having purchased it from your widowed mother. She described driving to the area for one last nostalgic look before the water flowed in. She found the house still standing, but to her horror, its porch had been ripped away, leaving its supports dangling bizarrely from the edge of the roof. She said they looked for all the world like "loose teeth wiggling in the wind." She spun her car around and drove away. She never looked back.

So, Grandpa, whenever I'm disheartened over another landmark from my youth disappearing from my hometown of

Calgary, I think of you losing your entire hometown. The actual event took place on *Dominion Day*, July 1, 1958—a date we now call *Canada Day*—when the great coffer-dam, originally created to provide a dry working environment for the project, was demolished, and the flooding began. In four days, 35,000 acres of prime land gurgled from sight. Takes your breath away, doesn't it? I have to say, I'm sort of thankful that you weren't here to bear witness. I was a student nurse at the time, trying to keep my head above water in a regimented program that left me little time for anything beyond my hospital world. I'm ashamed to admit how shockingly unaware I was of such a significant event taking place in my country, especially when it had a direct connection to my own family.

I have a photo of you as a single man, and I must say you cut a fine figure with that bushy bronze moustache. Beyond this photo, I only have patches of information to help me get to know you in your single days. I know that you were a telegrapher for the *Montreal Star*, which puts you in Montreal, of course. Telegraphy is such a specialized field. I've always wondered what drew you to it and where you learned your craft. Mother always talked about how close you were to your brother Clayton, who was just ahead of you in the Anderson pecking order. Clayton lived in Ottawa with his wife, Sadie, their two children, and Sadie's beautiful sister, Maria. I already know the conclusion to this part of your story, but I have one question before writing further: how many times did you travel the 125-mile stretch of railroad tracks between Montreal and Ottawa, before you eyed Sadie's sister in a new light? When she became more than your sister-in-law's sister? From my vantage, you didn't seem to be in any great rush to propose to Maria, because you waited until you were forty and she was thirty-eight. But you did it, and you and Maria were married in the beautiful new All Saints Anglican Church in Ottawa on June 8, 1901. It must have been a banner day, with your respective siblings, Sadie and Clayton, standing up for you. The Anderson brothers were now married to the Hall sisters. And aren't you glad that you lived long enough to witness the convention of sisters marrying brothers repeated in the next generation, when your two daughters, Mother and her sister Lillian, married the King brothers? Granted, the offspring are denied one whole set of cousins, but on the other hand, there's something special about having *double* cousins.

You and Maria, marrying in middle age, didn't leave a lot of room to produce children, but you were fortunate to have two healthy daughters without any complications. You chose interesting names for the girls, Ruby Loan Hall, my mother, and Sarah Lillian Whitney, her younger sister, my Aunt Lil. You gave Mother the surnames of her mother (Hall) and of her grandmother (Loan). Aunt Lil was named Sarah after Maria's beloved sister Sadie, while Whitney was the married surname of your sister, Mame, whose husband was George Whitney, brother of Sir James Pliny Whitney, premier of Ontario. Goodness, it took all my concentration to sort that one out! I'm told the senior Andersons made a habit of aggrandizing this remote connection to the premier, but I don't recall my aunt—Sarah Lillian Whitney—ever thinking her name was cause for celebrity. I do know, however, that Ruby Loan Hall took great pride in carrying the names of her very important family members.

To tell you the truth, Grandpa, I picture you a little confounded, going from forty years of bachelorhood to husband and father of two little girls in the blink of an eye. But that doesn't mean that you weren't proud as punch with your new status. In fact it's my understanding that the sun rose and set on the three *ladies* in your life, and you would have sailed along with the breeze at your back indefinitely ... had it not been for that dreadful day when the clouds rolled in. You were struck down with tuberculosis, a life-threatening diagnosis at that time. You must have been terrified. Little Ruby was only four years old and Lillian just an infant.

In August of that year, 1906, you travelled to a spa-type care centre north of Montreal called the Baths at Abenakis Springs for treatment. By October, you were admitted to *Dr. Kemp's Sanatorium* in Sainte-Agathe-des-Monts, located west of Abenakis in the Laurentians. Sainte-Agathe was relatively new, having been founded just seven years before you were there. Its site was selected for its fresh mountain air, considered by doctors as the best—if not *only*—hope for treating tuberculosis and other pulmonary diseases. Would you believe, Grandpa, that, half a century later, I worked at the *Baker Sanatorium* in Calgary as a student nurse, and, some years after that, at the *Aberhart Sanatorium* in Edmonton as a graduate nurse? I thought of you every day that I reported for duty at both locations. You'll be happy to learn that a cure was eventually discovered for TB, and by the late '60s sanatoriums across the country began closing. And this will bring a smile to your face: your Sainte-Agathe was converted into a popular recreation resort.

I have more good news. As you know, postcards were the main means of communication during this period, but what you may not know is that Mother treasured every card your family ever received, and carefully guarded the entire collection her whole life. Now in my hands, the cards tell me the story of your illness and the ultimate course of events to follow. It's especially touching to read the words of your colleagues at the *Montreal Star*: "Mr. Anderson, I am very glad to hear of you getting on so well and hope to hear of your coming back good and strong again." "Hello Mr. Anderson, How are you keeping?

Are you still gaining weight?" I am all too aware of weight loss with this disease, so gaining it back was foremost on everyone's mind as an indicator of restored health. But it's the postcards from you addressed to the family at their home at 824 Esplanade Avenue in Montreal (sometimes addressed as "Annex") that touch me the most. They truly bring home the reality of your extended separation from your beloved family, heart wrenching for all of you. Blessedly, beautiful Christmas postcards also turned up on Esplanade for all the family.

My heart soars when the new year—1907—arrives, and changes are revealed. Postcards for Grandmother and the little girls are now addressed to St. Agathe des Monts, indicating your family had moved to be near you. I never learned of this move until now, doubtless because Mother was too young to remember the fact. All these years later I find myself taking comfort in the knowledge that, after being sick and alone for such a long time, you now had your *ladies* close by, bringing sunshine to your days. The month of May brought even bigger changes for the family. But let's save that for another letter. I won't forget to write again soon.

Love you, Grandpa!
Your granddaughter,
Eleanor

Maternal Grandmother
Maria Hall Anderson

Born May 8, 1863—Richmond, Ontario
Died, May 10, 1924—Calgary, Alberta

Dear Grandmother,

I'll be honest, I have addressed my other grandmother as "Grandma," but I have a feeling that you would prefer the more formal "Grandmother." Mother always told me how proper you were, using the words *dignity* and *decorum* in any description of you. You also liked proper grammar, and no slang. The strange thing is, I'm not absolutely certain whether

I always addressed my mother formally as "Mother," but I rather think so, because I have certainly always referred to her as Mother. In any event, I love you wholeheartedly as my proper grandmother, and that's the way we'll keep it unless you signal otherwise.

One other thing: I absolutely love the way your name "Maria" is pronounced—<u>not</u> as in the *Sound of Music's*, "How do you solve a problem like Maria?" but rather as in *Paint Your Wagon's*, "They call the wind Mar<u>i</u>a." That's like a whole other name. Beautiful! And like your name, you were described as very beautiful; in fact, many suggested you held a strong resemblance to Queen Alexandra, queen consort of Edward VII. Is it any wonder family lore describes you as regal? Forgive the play on words, but since my name is King, that adjective could be assigned to me. But since there's never been a risk of that happening, you have regal all to yourself!

To be serious, Grandmother, I feel cheated that I never had you in my life, so I'm really keen to get to know you as I write. I do know that your father, John Hall, was a shoemaker, and your mother, Christina Moore Hall, was a wonderful seamstress. You had an older brother, two sisters—one older and one younger—and two little brothers. Early days in your family home might have been described as idyllic with you four older children lavishing attention on your two little brothers. Except tragedy struck. Within the space of one dreadful week, your father and the little boys all died suddenly. I believe it was assumed that they all succumbed to the same infectious disease or virus, a blow beyond imagining for those of you left behind. Your father was just thirty-six years old when he died, and you were a mere child of nine.

Your mother, in spite of overwhelming grief, bravely soldiered on, supporting her four surviving children with her exceptional skills as a dressmaker. Within the year, however, widowhood also prompted her to uproot the family from Richmond and move north to Ottawa, presumably to draw on support from her family. She quickly established her name as a much sought-after dressmaker in Ottawa. You were described as a sweet child, mature for your years, who willingly contributed to the running of the household from an early age. And you selflessly remained in the family home well into womanhood to lend support to your mother. Bless you.

In time, the oldest two, Julia and Will, married and left home, leaving you and your little sister Sarah (Sadie) alone with your widowed mother. I've been told that you and Sadie were like twins, strongly resembling one another and seemingly inseparable. The most outstanding feature that you shared with Sadie was your thatch of exceptionally curly hair. You know, of course, that you passed that along to your daughters. Once in a while, I could talk Mother into letting me roll her hair into large ringlets after she washed it so that I could watch the transformation as it dried—the ringlets tightening into little corkscrews. The curls passed on to me were not nearly as pronounced, but my daughter inherited your extra curly genes.

Sadie and Maria

Then a man entered your world of women; Clayton Anderson began courting your sister Sadie. Clayton was firmly established with the federal post office, having already served for seventeen years, when he met Sadie. Kind-hearted and mature, Clayton passed scrutiny, and after a respectable courtship period, he and Sadie were married. The newlyweds set up housekeeping on Ann Street in Ottawa, where they welcomed you and your mother. By all accounts, it was a harmonious household, and the arrival of a baby girl, Marge, completed the domestic scene. The only photos I have of Clayton, unearthed from Mother's haphazard collection box, reveal a portly, crusty-looking old guy in a rumpled suit, with a pipe, not my vision of someone living happily with four females in a three-generation household. I have to remind myself, of course, that he wasn't always old, and probably never crusty.

Three years after Marge's birth, the household was blessed with a baby boy, Earle, which pleased Clayton no end. Since your mother had died one year prior, after twenty-four years of widowhood, the family dynamics were now significantly altered. You remained in the household, revelling in your role as live-in aunt to your niece and nephew. As an adult, Earle used to say, in good humour, that he was known in the neighbourhood as *the little boy with two mothers*. I picture you—the *other mother*—tending to Sadie and Clayt's children with as much love and devotion as their real mother. Then one day, Reuben, Clayton's dashing younger brother from Montreal, began visiting … then more frequently.

You and Reuben were married, a small family wedding in Ottawa, with Sadie and Clayt as your attendants. You set up housekeeping in Montreal, which meant that at age thirty-eight, you and your beloved sister were living apart for the first time in your lives. The 125-mile separation must have felt beyond reach. And did Grandpa have any idea what a lucky guy he was, acquiring a bride who was already skilled at homemaking and childcare? I hope he didn't take you for granted. Men can be guilty of that sometimes.

You gave birth to Ruby, my mother, when you were thirty-nine, and Lillian when you were forty-three. When I was a student nurse on the maternity ward fifty years after you had Lillian, I remember being on high alert for increased risk of complications when an *elderly primipara* (a first pregnancy after the age of thirty-five) was admitted. But by all accounts, you carried out the whole proceeding with the same aplomb as you managed everything else. At least Mother never suggested otherwise, unless there were matters you never discussed with her. What I know for sure is that you produced two extremely bright little girls. I also know that, soon after Lillian's birth, life in your happy household was upended overnight, when Grandpa was struck down with tuberculosis.

You must have been devastated with this frightening diagnosis and the subsequent responsibilities that fell on your shoulders. Mother kept a collection of postcards the family received at the time, which has given me a glimpse into Grandpa's illness and the family's consequential movement. Cards were double postmarked—once at the post office of origin and again at their destination—sometimes the extra imprint maddeningly obscuring much of the message. Postage stamps were one cent.

The cards tell me that Grandpa first entered a sanatorium in August of 1906, where he stayed for nine months—such a long time. When he was discharged the end of April, his doctors recommended he "go west where the sun shines many days of the year and the air is dry." Calgary qualified. And so when he was strong enough, Grandpa boarded the train on his own, and journeyed west to seek work and living accommodations, while you and the girls moved in with Sadie and Clayt in their beautiful brick Ottawa home on Strathcona Avenue, to await word from Calgary.

Mother was just five years old during this hiatus, and as much as she missed her father, she became intensely attached to her Aunt Sadie and Uncle Clayton, and her *double* cousins, treasuring memories of this time together her whole life. Now, I regret that, when I was a child, I paid so little attention to Mother when she talked about her Aunt Sadie and Uncle Clayton. I scarcely even bothered to work out how they were related to her. It took me far too long to fully grasp how hugely important they were in her life, and how much she treasured them. Too late, I realized how much she missed their presence in her life, after the family moved west. I'm sure that, at the time, you grappled with conflicting emotions—sadness over your prolonged separation from Grandpa, but dread that re-joining him meant an indefinite separation from your beloved Ottawa family.

Grandpa's first en-route-to-Calgary postcard message was brief, "Just leaving Chapleau. 2 hours late, although good trip. Rube." I want to berate him for not doing better than that, then I remind myself that he was still recovering from a lengthy, merciless illness. He would have been anxious and exhausted. The following day, May 4, 1907, he seemed in better spirits, and was a bit more conversant: "We are nearing Port Arthur on Lake Superior. Lake covered with ice. We are in a first class sleeper to Winnipeg. Big snow storm last night. Sleeping fine. Love to all, Rube." I can only imagine the excitement when the May 6 postcard was delivered. "A few flakes of snow this am & pretty cold. Wearing heavy coat …" The card is postmarked Calgary! What I'm wondering, Grandmother, is whether  Grandpa's revelation that he's "wearing a heavy coat" is validation that he was looking after himself, or was he forewarning the family that Calgary in May could be cold? The photo on the front of this card, taken on the corner of Eighth Avenue and Centre Street, features horse and buggy.

The following day, a card addressed just to his little girl, Ruby, reads: "Hope you are getting on nicely & having a good time in Ottawa. Lots of flowers out here. Take good care of Lillian. Nice & warm here now. Dady [sic]." The front of this card carries a photo of *Central Public School* on Fifth Avenue and First Street Southwest, which had opened just two years prior—a glimpse into things to come for Ruby.

This is probably a good place to say goodbye for now. I'll save chatting about your new life in Calgary for next time.

I love you, Grandmother!
Your granddaughter,
Eleanor

—Chapter Two—
Great War Heroes

Introduction

Looking back on my early childhood during the Second World War, four connections to the war come to mind: food rations, blackout defence drills, my brother's collection of fighter airplane cards that he got out of *Crackerjack* candy popcorn boxes, and dark, depressing newsreels that accompanied feature movies in the theatres. The newsreels rolled out an exhaustive supply of bombs exploding in Europe, yet my young eyes still never fully grasped the magnitude of the war, or really what it was all about. I was cocooned in a warm, safe world—removed.

Now, in my eighties, I have been reaching farther back to an earlier war and my family's direct involvement with it. A full century has passed since WWI—the Great War—but the gap in time narrows as war records carry me back to my grandfather and two uncles slogging, wet and cold, through France's muck. After a lifetime harbouring remote images of trenches and battlefields, the horror of this war has become personal. Today, holding the military records of my three family members in my hands, I can trace their actual handwriting with my fingers. Now, I am addressing the everyday side of the war as it was for them. The questions flow—beyond combat, how did they manage everyday life in those ghastly trenches? How did they receive an adequate supply of food and water? How on earth did they manage the basic hygiene and sanitation that we take for granted? I shudder at the image of menacing vermin occupying the trenches alongside them, creating a daily routine of picking lice from their uniforms. How did they cope with constant fear and exhaustion? The ungodly sight of mates being blown apart before their eyes? How did they maintain their sanity in the midst of dead bodies piling up?

The statistics relating to the Canadian servicemen in the Great War are staggering. From a population of under eight million people, 619, 636 men enlisted or were conscripted. The King men were in good company: anywhere from two thirds to half the members of the Canadian Expeditionary Forces were British born. Close to 61,000 were killed, and thousands more died post war from complications of their wounds or related diseases. Countless men suffered from shell shock, a malady that was initially viewed as physical, caused by the concussing effects of constant shellfire on the brain. Later, when it was recognized that men were succumbing to an array of symptoms, running the gamut from nervousness to emotional collapse, or the complete slipping from the edge of sanity, it was recognized that shell shock encompassed both physical *and* mental wounds. The cumulative effects of terror in the trenches, prolonged warfare, crushing exhaustion, and the horror of mounting dead everywhere, were breaking even the strongest of men.

The Kings
On the Front

Grandpa King centre, standing.

Grandfather: Henry Clement King
Uncles: Arthur King and Walter King

Dear Grandpa,

Aunt Millie used to tell me that when the seven of you stepped onto Quebec soil for the first time in 1905, you did not consider yourselves immigrants—you were immediately Canadians. The fact that your adopted country was a fellow member of the British Commonwealth no doubt helped to make Canada feel like home. And the patriotic spirit that you brought with you made you the best Canadians.

Your patriotism is displayed—loud and clear—in a May 5, 1914, playbill that I have, announcing an "Empire Concert" at the Elite Theatre in Wainwright. The Union Jack and Canadian Red Ensign flags adorn the cover, and, inside, running along the bottom, it reads: "The proceeds are for uniforms—the uniforms are for the Cadets—the Cadets are for the Empire." Above that is the list of performers, your own five children cropping up frequently, whether it's your only daughter singing solo, or one of the boys playing the trumpet or the flute, reciting one of his own compositions, or presenting the flag. I know you would have been bursting your buttons over the contributions that your children made to the concert, but I suspect you were even more proud that all your sons were cadets.

One year later, on Thanksgiving Day, October 11, 1915, you outdid yourself by throwing a "Great Patriotic Banquet, Concert, and Dance" in the Elite Theatre. I visualize a grand affair with the whole town turning out for the celebration. There would have been mountains of turkey, mashed potatoes, and pumpkin pies, thanks to the women slaving for days in their kitchens. Meanwhile, you were whipping the performers into perfection with daily dress rehearsals. The day would not have been complete without a twirl on the dance floor with your teenage daughter, Millie, after your second helping of pumpkin pie. Much as her brothers adored her, I do not see one of them issuing her an invitation to dance. What, dance with my *sister*? When the day was done, you must have collapsed into bed exhausted, though elated with the success of the affair. But I'm betting that sleep did not come. By this time, news of the escalating war in your homeland was weighing heavily on your patriotic heart. The 151st (Central Alberta) Battalion unit of the Canadian Expeditionary Forces was beginning its recruitment campaign, and you knew you must answer the call. Within two months you had done so.

On December 6, 1915, you went to Edmonton to sign attestation papers to enlist in the Canadian Army. Research tells me that regulations of the time stipulated that enlistees had to be between ages eighteen and forty-five to serve. Records show that you listed your birth date as August 31, 1871, when I know that it was actually May 31, 1869. Ooh, Grandpa, you rascal! Got yourself just under the wire as a forty-four-year-old with that falsehood. Not only that, I'm told that you snuck off to Edmonton without telling your family, to avoid anyone running interference. They only learned what you'd done when you turned up in uniform. It's easy for me to forgive, knowing your patriotic motivation, but poor Grandma, what a shock that must have been for her. I have to smile at your answer to Question six on the form: What is your Trade or Calling? My bet is you didn't flinch when you wrote, "music teacher," in order to qualify as bandmaster. Well, Grandpa, whatever it takes. Besides, I don't doubt for a minute that you were fully capable to serve in that capacity. In fact, I'll bet the army never had a bandmaster to compare.

It's almost impossible for me to explain what a computer is (I should recruit my grandson Andrew for that task, because it's his specialty), but, loosely, it's a miracle invention of recent years that allows people all over the world to seek—or exchange—information with one another electronically, sort of through cyberspace. To my delight, I discovered that using this method, I could find your war records, preserved by the National Military Museum in Ottawa. My heart races when I see your own handwriting on your enlistment form—beautiful, artistic script.

You were recorded as 5'8" and 200 pounds. Ooh, Grandpa, do you think too much pumpkin pie? Still, the picture I have of you as bandmaster, standing front and centre with your band, suggests you carried that weight pretty efficiently, so I'm just going to view any extra pounds as more of you to love. I picture you with blue eyes and dark hair like all the Kings, but your records describe you with grey eyes and light hair. Perhaps your age—or the lighting—on that particular day created some subtle changes. Your two eldest sons enlisted shortly thereafter: Arthur, age twenty-one, and Walter, still seventeen, a few months shy of qualifications. Walter enlisted on December 7, 1915, in Wainwright, and Arthur about a month later, on January 3, 1916, also in Wainwright. All three of you were assigned to the 151st Battalion Canadian Expeditionary Forces and sent to Camp Sarcee in Calgary for your basic training. I only just learned through my sleuthing that during these Sarcee training days, the rest of the family—Grandma and the three younger children, Millie, seventeen, Harry, sixteen, and Horace, fourteen—packed up and moved to Calgary to be near the three of you.

This was the family's first exposure to Calgary, yet Dad never talked to us about this ten-month period in his life. For a lad of fourteen, it was no doubt an unsettling time, not something to store in his memory bank. But his big sister, Millie, had sketchy memories of the rental home and its location, details confirmed by your military records: The "Particulars of Family" page dated August 1916, indicated the family was living at 1924 - 27 Street West, Calgary, a district now known as Killarney. The little bungalow, rented from a Wainwright acquaintance, still stands. I find it touching that the family wanted to maintain close proximity to their servicemen in training. The mystery is how they managed financially, when the military stipend of the men rang in around a dollar a day each. Mind you, knowing the three teenagers in their later years, as I did, I'm certain that each one found a way to contribute to the welfare of all. And in spite of the obvious disruption to your lives and your apprehension about the future, I sense that the King family was now firmly of one accord: Calgary would always be home.

What I really wonder, Grandpa, is what was going through your mind as you filled out declaration forms:

> *"I, Henry Clement King, do solemnly dec'are … that I am willing to fulfil the engagements by me now made, and I hereby engage and agree to serve in The Canadian Over-Seas Expeditionary Force, and to be attached to any arm of the service therein, for the term of one year, or during the war now existing between Great Britain and Germany should the war last longer than one year, and for six months after the termination of that war provided His*

Majesty should so long require my services, or until legally discharged."

Did you have any perception of the horrors to come of this war? Or any expectations of how long it might last? Or, optimist that I believe you were, did you sign on the dotted line with the full conviction that you would not only survive this war, but you would emerge on the side of victory? The right side of history, as we say today. No one could have imagined that Canadian casualties would reach such unthinkable numbers: over 66,000 young men. Nor would you have imagined that one of your own—your beloved Arthur—would be among them.

The three of you set sail with twenty-nine officers and 925 soldiers of other ranks on the *S. S. California* from Halifax on October 3, 1916, disembarking in Liverpool, England, on October 13. You and Walter were absorbed by the 11th Battalion and Arthur by the 9th Battalion. From there you and Walter were sent to the vast military camp at Shorncliffe, staging post for troops bound for the Western Front in France. Arthur was sent to nearby St. Martin Plain. These two camps were just twenty miles across the English Channel from France, close enough that the sound of guns would have carried a grim reminder that a war was truly being waged nearby. The injured, arriving daily to the hospital at Shorncliffe, further brought home the sobering reality.

After two months in Shorncliffe, you and Walter sailed across the English Channel to France, where you joined the 5th Battalion on December 7, 1916. Arthur had preceded you to France by nine days, joining the 7th Battalion. When I read your records, I see that, as bandmaster, you were likely billeted in homes that spared you from life in the trenches. But that doesn't mean that you escaped the consequences of muddy battlefields and inclement weather. In fact, three hospitalizations with bronchitis tell me that you were waging war on two fronts, one being your own health. And that war didn't end with the armistice; your final medical report gives me chills. In May 1919, while you were awaiting return assignment to Canada, you were admitted to hospital a fourth time, diagnosed with the infamous 1918 'flu, which killed millions. Considering the weakened state of your lungs, your survival was miraculous.

You might be surprised to learn that a clump of postcards written by you while you were billeted in a private home in Mazingarbe has survived. Many were never posted, which leads me to believe that perhaps you wrote them as a journal. You describe the devastation of a string of small coal mining towns: "The great slag heaps like mountains thrown up out of the mines." You feared for the safety of your band: "German shells are thrown randomly into the town all the time." You spent the coldest part of 1917 in and around the town of Bully-les-Mines, where you described, "Playing the Battalion out of the trenches in the town on a wintry day in January." You had grown attached to the town and its people, and I could feel your heartache as you added, "Bully has practically been smashed to pieces."

But your postcards were not all doom and gloom. Two in particular refreshingly suggest that you escaped the shelling long enough to explore the local culture. One from Noeux-Les-Mines reveals the jeweller and art connoisseur in you: "Quite a large town of about 9,000 people. Walter and I walked through to see *R.S.M. Haydin* at the Brigade Service—a distance of 16 kilometres return. Visited a fancy store, priced some vases of fall leaves and fruit under glass cases—a very popular thing among the mining population. Beautiful country, good crops growing right up to the town."

You signed this card formally: H. C. King. July 16, 1917. Bandmaster 5th Canadian Battalion. And from the town of Olhain, if I didn't know better, I might have thought you were simply a tourist: "Grenez district, a very old Chateau surrounded by a moat with draw bridge. Visited all through the place with Mr. A. Franzen—the basement showing wine cellars and the tower giving a splendid view of the country." I gasped when I read the postscript you added to the bottom of this card: "The 7th Battalion passed up about 4 o'clock. We saw Arthur march." Did you write that with a lump in your throat, Grandpa?

When I pore through the military records of the three of you, I can only conclude that this was the one and only time that you saw Arthur after parting company in Liverpool to join your separate battalions. You never saw him again. Oh Grandpa, you must have replayed that scene of him time and again for the rest of your life: Arthur marching away with his unit. And that begs the question: how soon after Arthur was killed were you informed of his death? And where were you at the time? Did you receive the news from Walter, or, heaven forbid, did you find Arthur's name on one of those impersonal casualty lists compiled daily? I wish I could take comfort in knowing that the news was broken to you gently by some kindly chaplain offering a prayer, but in that ungodly war, I have my doubts.

Finally, I have to confess that I never really addressed the particulars of demobilizing troops after the war. I just sort of pictured you all getting on a boat and heading for home. Now that I've finally come to my senses, I recognize the complexity of the massive operation. The wonder is, how on earth it was all managed. I learned that you were in a Discharge Depot for some months before your time came. It's here that you were hospitalized in the military hospital in Bramshott with the 'flu, which was rapidly becoming the scourge of the veterans. On June 21, 1919, you set sail for the return to Canada on the *R. M. S. Minnedosa*, embarking in Liverpool and disembarking in Quebec on July 2. You received your final discharge papers in Quebec on July 7, 1919. You had survived serious illness and escaped death on the Front—you were safe on Canadian soil. Your were home.

Well, I guess that's about it for now. Oh, just one more thing: I hope this pleases you as much as it does me. Do you remember the large shells that you brought back from France? The ones you painted with beautiful flowers on a deep green background? I don't know what you called such items back then, but we refer to them now as *trench art*. Well, your *trench vases* filtered through the family to me somehow, and they're gracing the front hall table in my home. I love them.

They are conversation pieces to be sure, but what I love most is their abiding reminder of you. What could be better than that?

Love,
Eleanor

Arthur King

Born November 21, 1894—Preston, Lancashire, England
Killed in Action April 19, 1918—France

Dear Uncle Arthur,

I sort of pinch myself addressing you as *Uncle* Arthur, when I never really experienced you as an uncle. Conversely, you never experienced *being* an uncle. But the fact remains, we are uncle and niece, and that's kind of special, don't you think? So before I get started, I'll clarify our connection: I am the youngest of the youngest, daughter of your little brother Horace.

The family spoke of you often, especially your only sister, my Aunt Millie, who sang praises of you. She adored all four of her brothers, but she always looked up to you as the responsible big brother that she could trust to look out for her. In a family of practical jokers, it would have been reassuring to have one ally. Since I have no way of discerning your personality, I have looked to my dad and my other uncles, Walter and Harry, to conjure up a picture of you. The one thing they had in common was a wicked sense of humour, suggesting to me that this is an inborn trait of the King brothers. Whenever the gang gathered, you wouldn't believe the antics. We'd laugh the entire time we were together, and I always believed that if you'd been with us, the sound would have escalated a decibel or four. Thinking of you amongst us brings me pure joy.

Then I turn to your military records, and the laughter and joy abandon me. You had just turned twenty-one when you enlisted in Wainwright, on January 3, 1916. You had earned a teaching certificate from Normal School in Calgary, and you were establishing yourself as a teacher in Edgerton, a small community east of Wainwright. And you had a special girl, Marguerite. The world was your oyster. I blink back the tears when I read the page headed:

> Perforated sheet for Will from Pay Book of :
> Reg. No. 624249
> Name Arthur King
> Unit 7th Canadian Batt.B.E.F.
>
> Military Will
> In the event of my death I give the whole of my property and effects to my mother, Mrs. H. C. King... .

I try to imagine your frame of mind as you filled out this page. It must have been the first time you ever even addressed the possibility of your own mortality. Twenty-one-year-old guys typically think they're indestructible. Suddenly, I become thankful that I have lived in a time when the men in my life—my husband, brothers, and sons—never had to face a call to serve. It's not lost on me that you fought and died for them. What price freedom?

I confess that I know little about military rank and file, but your enlistment records show that you were appointed to acting sergeant at the outset. I'm guessing this was in recognition of your service as a lieutenant in the Canadian Militia back in Wainwright, where you were also a cadet instructor. When you disembarked from the *S. S. California* on October 13, 1916, at Liverpool, England, could you ever have imagined returning to your homeland under these circumstances? You must have longed to take a side trip to Preston, your old hometown, but there was no time for such frivolities. You were immediately transferred to the 9th Reserve Battalion at St. Martin's Plain, the military training facility located on the southeast coast, bordering the English Channel. Exactly one month later, November 12, 1916, the entry on your Active Service Form reads, "Reverts to the ranks at own request to proceed overseas." When I read that I want to cry out, "No, Private King, no! Don't be in a hurry to go overseas!" But the military take you at your word, and on that same date, you are transferred to the 7th Battalion Overseas.

One day later, you arrive at the National Regimental Depot in France, and a week after that, December 1, you have joined your battalion in the field. I know that as a Canadian you had experienced tough winters, but always with a warm home and a hot meal at the end of the day. Now I'm trying to picture you in France, facing the chill of December, with no prospects for the warmth of home and family.

Then your records become sparse—just six more entries spanning eighteen months of service, which scarcely gives me an inkling of your circumstances during that time. I have a handful of postcards and letters written from the front by the King men, but, unfortunately, only one from you. I guess you were a man of few words. Your lone card, pencilled on December 3, 1916, from Villers-Au-Bois in the north of France, states, "Marched up here from Aubigny. Left Dec. 26, 1916. A. King." You really were a man of few words, weren't you? The card tells me that you spent Christmas there, but little else, except when I look up the two said villages on a map, I discover the distance between them is over 300 kilometres. That was a long march. Researching Villers-Au-Bois, I see that it is located in the department of Pas-de-Calais, a geographically strategic area between England and Germany. You were undeniably in the thick of it there.

Over the course of the next year, you endured life in the trenches, which meant filth and deprivation, and death dogging you daily. Some describe that war as unmitigated butchery. As I read more about that war, knowledge does not bring me comfort, but it does bring me understanding. And it brings me ever closer to you. I have learned that many of the men suffered from shell shock, its debilitating symptoms a direct consequence of the war. Added to the nightmare of battling this alarming condition was the distrust of its validity by many, even in the medical profession. Such a view was like rubbing salt in the wound. I hope the world is doing better at understanding the psychological wounds of war now, but I have a feeling we still have a long way to go with accepting and treating it.

The one entry on your record that brings me joy is entered by a stamp on December 8, 1917: GRANTED 14 DAYS LEAVE. My elation doubled on discovering that your brother Walter, with the 5th Battalion, was granted the same two weeks. Home to Preston to celebrate an early Christmas with the family. I have pored over Grandpa's records hoping to find that he, too, was on leave that Christmas. I've read the 1917 entries up and down, forward and backward, as if willing it to be, but, alas, his was the one empty chair at the Christmas dinner table that year. So I content myself with a vision of Grandma and your sister, Millie, preparing a feast for their men, while you and Walter roughhouse with your younger brothers. I want to put that vision on a long pause, but I'm drawn back to the military records and the rest of the war story. Records show that Walter reported back for duty on December 22, following his allotted fourteen days, but you did not return for another week, December 29. My fear is that you were not well, which would not be surprising. Do you know how much I wish that you had never returned?

On Friday, the nineteenth of April, 1918, you were killed during a lull in combat by shrapnel from a bomb landing near the mouth of your dugout. You were just twenty-three years old. Walter was called over to care for you. He took possession of your valuables, and wrapped you in a blanket for burial. You rest in Roclincourt Cemetery in France, where the French have been lovingly tending your grave ever since. Walter reeled when he found the photo of your beloved Marguerite in your chest pocket, shrapnel piercing her face. Your suffering was over, but for the rest of the family it was just beginning. You have been mourned forever after. I have never become immune to the horrors of the Great War, and never dismissed the King family's great loss. One day, in conversations with my cousin Audrey (Harry's youngest), her response to the shared loss of our *unknown soldier*, was uncomplicated and touching: "We should have known Arthur," she said matter-of-factly. Yes, we should have. I hope I'm at least getting to know you a little, as I chat with you today.

Getting to Know You

In closing, Uncle Arthur, it goes without saying that your nieces and nephews carry you in our hearts, but I want you to know that, additionally, your name is carved for posterity on a number of memorials, which I have made a special point of visiting: on your parents' gravestone in Preston, on Canada's breathtaking War Memorial at Vimy, France, and on a touching stone monument in Wainwright. More recently, Calgary volunteers have been installing a major expanse of crosses in a field on Memorial Drive every November, the month when we *remember* our soldiers who gave their lives. Arthur King is on one of those crosses. So you see, you are not forgotten, and never will be.

Well, I guess that's about it. I'm going to write Uncle Walter next. You'll be pleased to know that he was also my godfather. I was blessed to have him in my life, but it wasn't long enough to know him well. He died of a heart attack just five days before I became a teenager. I'm hoping that as I wade through his war records, maybe I'll get to know him better.

Love you, Uncle Arthur!
Your niece,
Eleanor

P. S. Our *Maclean's* magazine published an amazing Centennial Commemorative Issue in November 2018. I made sure *Maclean's* remembered you, too!

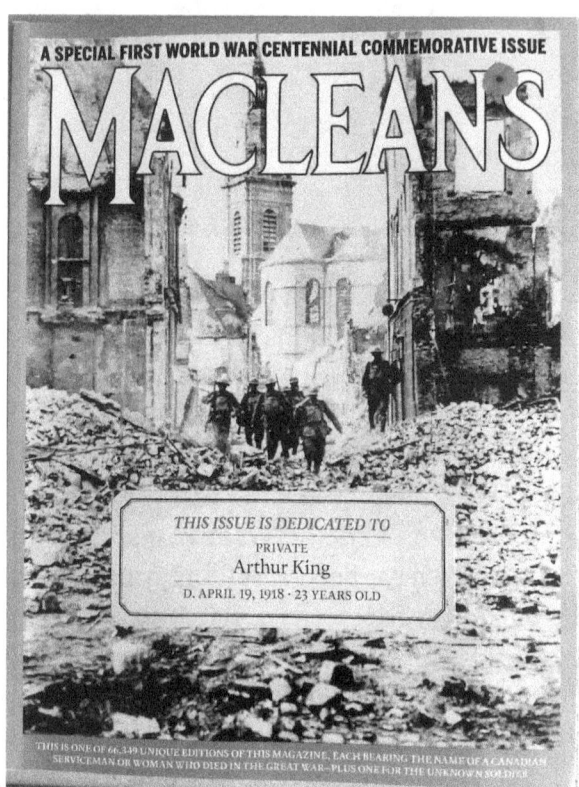

Walter King

Born January 3, 1898—Preston, Lancashire, England
Died September 17, 1950—Calgary, Alberta, Canada

Dear Uncle Walter,

It's just occurring to me that my memories of you almost entirely take place in the big living room of your Elbow Park home. We're playing games—Tip It, McGillicutty, charades—and I see the hilarity building with your inventive add-ons. You were never content to play a game in the same unimaginative way that others would. Do you remember calling your own version of BINGO? "Under the O Clickity Click"—or—"O Top of the House." By the time Cousin Frank explained to me what each innovation was, you had called two more numbers. No wonder I never won.

My other memory of you is reciting poetry. I was dumbfounded by the length of poems you could memorize. *Kissing Cups Race* was 144 lines. How on earth? And of course, you also wrote poetry. Your most famous was *The Fight For Vimy Ridge*, which you once performed in an amateur contest at the Grand Theatre. You won first prize! Which brings me to the Great War, something I've had on my mind a lot lately. You served overseas with your father and brother, but you're the only one that I had the opportunity to know. The thing is, I never heard you breathe a word of your war experience, which I understand is not uncommon—a code of silence seems to be the norm amongst soldiers who fought. And here I am, 100 years after the fact, wanting to talk about it. I hope you don't mind.

Firstly, it's my understanding that, because of your young age, you were not sent into combat, but rather assigned as stretcher bearer, which scarcely protected you from personal injury, never mind the horrors of witnessing catastrophic injuries and death all around you. On some of your war records you have referred to yourself as "Bandsman" Walter King, with every indication that you additionally participated in your father's band on occasion. I know that you played the drums, but I wouldn't be surprised to learn that you picked up one or more of the horns. Of the three family members who served, you were the most prolific letter writer, and I can't tell you how thankful I am that your family preserved your letters, written from the Front. Nothing brings the war more alive for me. My hope now is to get to know you better, by bouncing your own words back to you.

Your first letter to your mother, written when you had only been in France for a month, takes my breath away. It paints such a vivid picture. You had just turned nineteen.

"Somewhere in France, Jan. 26, 1917.

Dear Mother. I received your letter of the 18th today. Your last parcel seemed to have come quite quickly for it got here with my birthday parcel. You certainly have done well to send all that out. I think we are pretty well fixed up now for some time, but anytime you are sending anything out to Father or me, slip a refill for my stove in. I usually make a cup of coca ... to warm up before going to bed.... .

It is very cold here and the ground is covered with snow. Everything is frozen up. The sky is clear, both day and night, so Fritz's aeroplanes are out again. There was one today right above us, but he was very high. A British warplane went up after him, but it took him a long time to gain such height. He had to go up in spirals and by the time he got there, Fritz was beating it in the other direction. I don't think our airman knew he had gone for he kept flying around in a circle as though he were looking for him, but the anti-aircraft guns had spotted him and gave him several shots to scare him off.

We are billeted in a barn again right in the town. The people of the house allow us to sit in the kitchen by the fire while it is so cold. We expect the weather to break up soon. Our men are all in the trenches now, and we are busy getting up a Pierrot concert for when they come out. They are four days in, and four out. I suppose Father will be telling you all about it.

At first we thought we were going to be billeted in a proper house in the next town, one kilometre away, so we were disappointed when we heard we had to move here. However, a 10th Battalion man was telling me tonight that our famous billet was "knocked to pieces" by a German shell yesterday.

I got a Xmas card from Mr. & Mrs. Aykroyd, and a box of chocolates from the children. The roads are hard now, so it is much easier to move artillery about.

I don't think there is anything more to tell you just now. With best of love to all—and every confidence in British success this year—your son, Walter."

Three months later, you sound like a seasoned veteran as you describe the stark reality of your days. Your pride in the Canadians is palpable. So, too, is your admiration for the number of Germans who spoke English. (Maybe that had something to do with your mission to speak both German and French by the end of the war, which you accomplished.) There is no disguising your casual request for a "good pair of socks" tacked on at the end of your letter; in fact, it would have been a plea for a much longed-for item in your wardrobe. Warm socks from home—manna from heaven.

<u>"Somewhere in France, April 16, 1917.</u>

Dear Mother. I guess it is about time I sent a line home again. I had not had a letter from Preston for a good many days now.

I suppose father will have been telling you that we have been sent up the line the last few days so have had no time to ourselves. You will see by the papers too of the big fight of the Canadians. Perhaps Germany will sit up and take notice if she gets a few more smashes.

We had quite a few casualties, but nothing compared with the German losses. Their own official report announces the smash up of two divisions, over 30,000 men. Many were killed, a lot wounded, but the majority taken prisoner.

When the fight was over the street was lined with hospital transports waiting to get into the hospital. I was helping to carry the stretchers in for a while. The German wounded were mixed right in with ours, and were treated alike. What surprises me most is the number of them that can speak English.

The next afternoon we went up the line, past our old front line trenches, over "no man's land" and right into the old German support lines. Our artillery was firing over our heads all the time Fritz shelled us a little, but our artillery was so active that he thought it best to quit.

The land was in an awful mess. There was not a yard of level ground left, for it is just one mass of shell holes, and huge mine craters. We were out until half past one in the morning collecting waste ammunition and carrying up water to the trenches. We had some time getting home in the dark and went quite a long way round, tripping over wire entanglements and slipping in shell holes and trenches full of water. My puttees are pretty well ripped to pieces.

Two days later we went up again. It is about seven or eight miles from here so the walk there and back was quite a stunt. We started at 5:30 in the morning and got back about 9:30. We were off at the same time next day and got back at about 5 o'clock. At six the same day we got orders to pack up and move out. We went about a mile and waited there for further orders which were supposed to come, but never did, so had to go back and sleep on the floor of the town hall.

Now that we have pushed the Germans back, we will have to move further on. Our big guns are moving up all the time.... So where is the famous Hindenburg Line now?

I have not seen an instrument for some days now. I guess we'll all be pretty well out of practice by the time we get at them again. We are all quite well and, to put it all in a nutshell, are having a "whale of a time." Hope this finds you all well at home. A good pair of socks would be appreciated. Walter."

Two days later, the brutality is more evident as you describe burying seventy-two comrades from your own battalion. I can't imagine a nineteen-year-old kid living through such trauma.

"*France, April 18, 1917.*

Dear Mother, Got your letter of the 12th today. So you know in England that we have taken Vimy Ridge. I see by tonight's paper that we are now fighting in the suburbs of Lens. If we capture that we will have done something, for the population in peacetime was 32,000. We got Lievin with 25,000 yesterday. Once we get them out of the trenches the rest will be easy picking. Large bodies of cavalry have been passing through here lately, so they must be getting ready to chase them up when the infantry start them running.

The papers will show you the importance of Vimy Ridge, supposed to have been the Kaiser's greatest stronghold on this front. Many divisions of French troops have fallen trying to take it when they held that part of the line.

A German sergeant-major taken prisoner said to the fellows, "Comerads, you take Vimy Ridge, you win the war."

Besides carrying up ammunition and water supplies ... we were sent up on a burying party. We buried (72) 5th Battalion men, but the dead Fritzs lying around was a terror. Nearly every dug-out was piled up with them.

... Major Lowery had two fingers blown off his left hand, one off his right, was shot in the left thigh with shrapnel, in the left foot with shrapnel, and sniped in the right knee as he was being carried out on the stretcher.... .

Father was over and looked at the 7th Bn. casualties after the big fight, but Arthur's name wasn't there so he must be all right. The 7th are not here now, but we will see them again in a few days... . Best wishes to all at home. Walter."

The thought of your father checking the 7th Battalion casualty list "after the big fight" to see if Arthur's name is on it, gives me chills. Obviously, not finding Arthur's name would have brought great relief, yet it in some way, small comfort—he could not ignore the countless names that were on the list. So many sons. So many mourning fathers.

And finally, your dramatic letter of November 11, 1918. But then, you can't over-dramatize such a consequential day. Everything is on display in this letter—your grasp of the magnitude of the war, your perception of the enemy, justification for your victory, and, touchingly, your support for your mother in sacrificing Arthur for the cause. You grew to manhood on the battlefront. You were already taking your place as oldest son—big brother to the three siblings in Preston awaiting your return.

"<u>Somewhere in France, Nov. 11th, 1918.</u>

Dear Mother. The great European war is over! All last night we expected the news to come through, but we did not know officially until 10 o'clock this morning that the armistice had been signed. No doubt London, Paris, Washington and Rome are seething with excitement at the conclusion of the world's greatest struggle, but there are no celebrations of any kind here tonight. Probably it is because most of the boys cannot yet realize that what they set out to do has been accomplished, yet apart from all that there are really no means of celebrating here. It is raining out, and the town is dead quiet. Today we had a general inspection and stood out six hours in the cold rain. Parades are going on as usual, and it appears as though the period of demobilization is only going to leave everyone with a more bitter memory of army life than is necessary.

I received two letters from you today, and am glad to hear you talk the way you do. Now that everything is over I have a few things to say. I need not dwell on any of my own previous remarks on the termination of the war. You may think what you wish of those, but events have proved my words. To you and Uncle Walter, the only two British relatives I own, there must have arisen, as there has to me, a great victory from more than one point of view. As for the rest, they will know more of what I think of them when next we meet, and the thought must flash through their minds.... To those who still credit the German nation with being clever I pity them.... What about the boys who were holding on against overwhelming odds in the spring, while these people in England were admiring the cleverness of the Hun? What about the boys who were fighting their way through Cambrai, while the people at home were saying, "You'll never get through the Hindenburg Line—you've got a hard nut to crack this time, etc!" That was splendid support, wasn't it? Just over four years is a marvellously short time to finish a war of this nature, but it would never have lasted this long if everyone at home had been like you and Uncle Walter, and at the termination of it all it is some consolation to know that the great sacrifice made by Arthur and the many others has not been for nothing. You yourself have done all that could be expected... and much more. Arthur and I often spoke of that together out here and since he has gone, hard though it has been ... I am glad to say you never once doubted the success of the cause for which Arthur gave his life.... With heartfelt thanks for all you have done for us, and hoping to be home again soon. Your affectionate son, Walter."

Your records then show that you received fourteen days' leave the following month, which allowed time in Preston with the family. I'll bet your mother never wanted to let you out of her sight again. But she had to; it wasn't quite over yet. You were required to rejoin your unit at a Discharge Depot to await embarkation orders back to Canada. You finally set sail on April 2, 1919, and landed on Canadian soil on April 10, some three months ahead of the rest of the family. You received your final discharge papers in Quebec on April 24. From there, you travelled to Calgary on your own, where you set about finding living quarters for the family, soon to follow. It was over at last. Or was it?

I've read that returning soldiers are forever changed by the war. How could it be otherwise? You brought home with you nightmares of atrocities that most of us can't conceive. On March 28, 1918, you caught a glimpse of Arthur, as his battalion marched past yours in a rainstorm. Three weeks later, he was dead. The story is heartbreaking enough, without the added cruelty of a thoughtless mate—hardened by death—callously calling out to you, "Hey, King! Your brother needs you over there." You stumbled over the rubble of destruction in the direction he indicated, only to find Arthur lying among the dead. No kind chaplain bringing you the news and offering a prayer, was there? Kneeling in a wasteland of carnage, you tended to your big brother by taking possession of his valuables and tenderly wrapping him in a blanket for burial. Your final goodbye took place the next day, when you buried him in nearby Roclincourt Military Cemetery. Did anyone come to comfort you? Or was everyone by now desensitized to death? Just another day. Another body. If there's any comfort to be found in this story, it's that Arthur was tended by his loving brother on his final journey.

In 1936, you led a group of Canadian veterans on a pilgrimage to France for the unveiling of the breathtaking Canadian National Vimy Memorial, honouring Canadians who gave their lives in the Great War. A highlight of this trip was visiting the billeting towns, staying one night with the family that had billeted you during the war. Memories of this kind family remained with you forever, as did your fluency in French, which you learned at their dinner table. The family's daughter, Annie Duquesne, corresponded with you in Redcliff after the war. In one letter, she told you about her contribution to the Second World War as a member of the French underground.

In the book, *The Secret History of Solders*, author Tim Cook speaks of poetry being written as an emotional outlet by men "standing in trenches and rubbing whale oil on their feet to keep their toes from rotting off." The appalling conditions, he explained, was a reason poems were often "juvenile and simple." He also reminds us that the average education of the enlisted man was Grade 6. Well, Uncle Walter, he was not describing you. You had won gold medals for academic standing in junior and senior high schools, silver medals for perfect attendance, and top awards for best officer in the Wainwright Cadet Corps. As if that wasn't enough, you completed Grade 12 and earned a teaching certificate from Normal School by the age of sixteen—so young, in fact, the board of education withheld it from you until after the war—and then only when you threatened action from the Canadian Legion. You showed them!

But I got sidetracked—back to the "juvenile and simple" poems that Tim Cook talked about. He certainly didn't see your poem, *The Fight for Vimy Ridge*, which flies in the face of *simple*. Of course you composed it after the war, not while in the trenches rubbing your feet. I'm pretty sure you could recite it backward in your sleep, but I'm going to tack it onto my letter in any event so we can both see it in print once again. I'm drawn to the history lesson it offers, as you honour the British and French allied forces, while revealing special pride in the Canadians:

THE FIGHT FOR VIMY RIDGE

PROLOGUE
What are the lights behind the hill
That upwards shoot throughout the night?
Why do those minute balls of fire
Rise up incessantly to light
The Vimy Ridge?

What is the rumble plainly heard
Over the hills low summits drear?
Why has that awful noise boomed forth
Unceasingly throughout the year
On Vimy Ridge?

What means those crosses on the hill
Those wooden crosses bleak and bare?
Why are those thousands side by side
In rest upon the hillside there
On Vimy Ridge?

What do they mean those signs afar?
Surely they have a tale to tell?
Then listen and you all shall know
Of how the German stronghold fell,
The Vimy Ridge.

THE STAND AT VIMY
The Campaign of 1914

The Allied line in full retreat from Mons
Had learnt at awful cost their need of guns;
The men were heroes all and bravely fought
But man against machinery counts as naught.

Quite unopposed now that our troops had gone
Flower of the Prussian Army followed on
The road to France's capital seemed clear,
A stand at Calais was their only fear.

But if they thought that such was France's fate,
Then they were doomed to disappointment great;
For soon they saw not far across the land
The long, thin khaki line had made a stand.

Instead of showing fight the Huns then backed,
The great would-be attackers were attacked;
They soon retreated when their plans went wrong,
And chose for their positions Vimy strong.

THE FRENCH ATTACK
The Campaign of 1915

The French had drawn the sword from out its sheath
Relieved the British of their post of death
Their's was a fight like France ne'er fought before
'Twas for existence and not merely war.

And thus it was the foe they went to meet,
Knowing full well the meaning of defeat;
Charge followed charge through drenching rain and mud
But every yard gained was bought with blood.

Yet Neville did not mean to be thrown back,
He massed his troops for one supreme attack;
Six hundred guns lined Vimy Ridge that night,
All ready for the big ensuing flight.

The fight, the French relate with remorse,
The Huns still held the Vimy Ridge in force;

It seemed impregnable that fortress there,
And so was given up in deep despair.

THE BRITISH ATTACK
The Campaign of 1916

The British line moved further south next spring,
Relief to France's weary men they bring;
They had a new attack in view that year,
The time for Vimy's fall was drawing near.

For all the guns massed there by France before
Were nothing to the implements of war
With which the British knocked at Vimy's gate
They knocked, and hard; but did it much too late.

Before the ridge was taken winter came,
The Huns had held their own in that campaign;
But when spring dawned on Vimy's ridge so clear,
Canadians faced the foe to try a year.

Line after line of British monster guns
Were there with ample shells to give the Huns,
For 'twas over the top with the best of luck,
When morning dawned for "Johnny Canuck."

THE FALL OF VIMY
Canadian Attack 5:30 am April 9, 1917

"Stand-to," the men got orders all that night,
And—Charge as soon as ever it was light;
So up the ridge they scramble, going higher,
Backed by the world's best barricade of fire.

Stormed at in front, and shelled to bits behind,
Blown in the air on ground where it was mined;
Bombed from their dug-outs, caught on every side,
The Huns had not a single place to hide.

Thousands surrendered, those who dare retire
Were mown down by the British line of fire;
Vimi had "fallen," Hindenburg's great plans
Were crushed to earth—The ridge that day changed hands.

So this is how Canadians made their name,
Teaching the Germans how to "play the game";
And all our losses in the Vimy fight,
They were repaid in full that Easter night.

CONCLUSION

What are the lights like rockets sent,
That upwards shoot, both green and white?
Just starshells from the German lines,
In fear of an attack by night
O'er Vimy Ridge.

What is the rumble plainly heard
Over the hills we see afar?
Why 'tis the boom of British guns
Playing their part in this great war
On Vimy Ridge.

What means those crosses on the hill,
Those wooden crosses did you say!
They mark the graves of those who fell
In freedom's cause; to win the day
On Vimy Ridge.

Getting to Know You

When Britons boast of Marlborough,
Or Wellington at Waterloo;
Well may they pause Sir Douglas Haig
To pay a compliment to you
For Vimy Ridge.

Composed by Bandsman Walter King 624037,
5th Battalion, **B.E.F** *France*

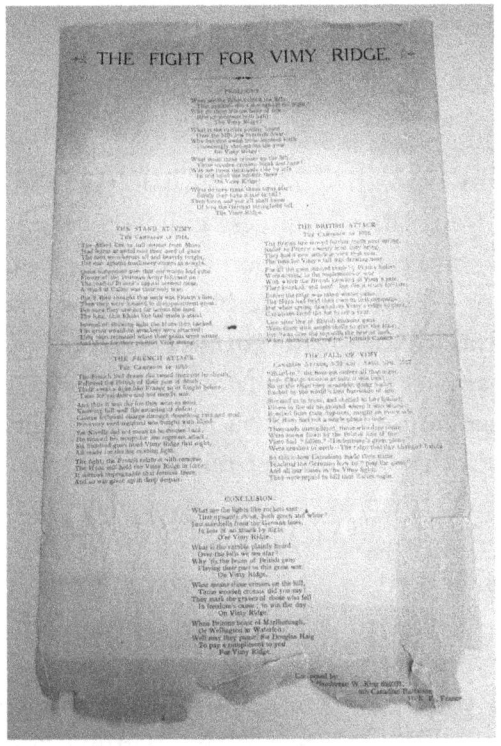

Well, this is probably a good place to stop for this time. I'll write again soon!

Much love,
Eleanor

Brave Backers
Grandma King
Aunt Millie
Uncle Harry
Horace—Father

Dear Grandma,

You are my hero. Imagine just packing up and sailing the ocean with your three youngest children to set up housekeeping back in Preston, so that you could be near your men on the Front. What a wonderful show of support. I have made a special trip to Preston to seek out some of the family landmarks, among them, 253 Manchester Road, the address of the terrace house, where you lived during the war years. I've been told that your Potter relatives lived just across the way, so it's good to know that the trying war years were made a little easier for you, with their support.

Aunt Millie used to stress that you not only maintained your home as a safe haven for your family and welcome retreat for your warriors on leave, but that you made it known that your door was open to other soldiers on leave also, especially Canadians that were battling homesickness. Many of these young men were experiencing separation from their families for the first time. You loved them all, I know, but Aunt Millie used to hint that the boys from Wainwright found a special place in your heart, and you treated them like guests of honour. Your meals would have been legendary, Grandma. Imagine a visiting soldier's bliss, diving into a plate of your heavenly roast beef and Yorkshire pudding, piled high with mashed potatoes and gravy, after months scarcely getting by on military rations of canned bully beef and bone-dry biscuits.

Aunt Millie described the house as having two sitting rooms, a large one used by the family, and a smaller one that you reserved for special visitors, such as the local minister. Soldiers on leave unequivocally fell into the *special* category. As I look back over a century after that horrifying war, the only palatable image I can conjure is that of your warm, nurturing home awaiting our brave servicemen. Thank you for that.

When I think of Christmas 1917, my heart breaks. You would have celebrated a few days early, to accommodate the granted leaves of Arthur and Walter. Grandpa was not with you; his granted leave came after Christmas. I picture your boisterous sons gathered around the table, while you and Millie served them a scrumptious turkey dinner with every trimming you could scrounge. I hope sugar rationing didn't get in the way of you making some of your famous Goosnargh cakes. And of course, you'd never let a Sunday pass without visiting your beloved church, to give thanks for your family and for your Canadian troops, and to pray for their safety. I'd like to think that before time ran out, the guys may have indulged in a cockamamy game of McGillicutty, but somehow I doubt they were in the right frame of mind for such nonsense.

My heartwarming vision is shattered by the knowledge that, when your two young warriors departed from this joyous setting, only one would return. Less than four months later, Arthur would die on the muddy fields of France. You would be denied all the farewell rituals we normally award such a parting: a final goodbye kiss, a funeral service with all the honours, and witness to his casket being lowered into its grave. You had nothing to help you come to terms with this terrible loss. Arthur just went away. How does one deal with that? I weep for you.

I too, have lost a son, Grandma, under wholly different circumstances, but heartbreaking nevertheless. I'm a believer that no one knows a young man like his mother. Somehow, I feel certain that poor Arthur suffered from shell shock at that time, an all-too-prevalent infliction suffered by troops on the front. Unfortunately, because of its mystifying aspect, doctors were challenged to treat it with any degree of success. Arthur's *hidden* injuries may have escaped the eye of many around him, but not you. I can only imagine the anguish you experienced after sending him off to the Front again.

You will also know, as I have learned, that remorse travels hand in hand with grief. You would have spent sleepless nights asking yourself what you might have done differently: "Was he getting the medical help he needed?" "Why did I trust the military doctors to care for him?" "Was he fit to serve when I sent him off?" "What cost freedom?" Then questions of disquieting minutiae drag on and on: "In the flurry of sending him off, did I expressly tell him I loved him?" "Was he frightened leaving home that last time?" "Was there a buddy tending him when he died? Before Walter reached his side?" "Was he cold?" "Did I pack enough warm socks?" "What were his final thoughts?" I know all the questions, Grandma. I have asked every one of them myself. Neither of us witnessed the end for our sons—we can only surmise how it came about. But of this I am sure, as they closed their eyes, they knew their mother's love.

While still battling the crushing fatigue that accompanies grief, you set about demobilizing and preparing for your return to Canada. I would ask if you were ever tempted to stay put in your homeland amongst your Potter family, except I already know the answer. You had become a dyed-in-the-wool Canadian; you were going home. And this time, home would be Calgary, the city you had grown to love. Walter had evidently gone ahead and found living accommodations at 812 - 3rd Avenue West. Knowing how energetic and resourceful he was, I imagine him scraping together some furniture and pots and pans in readiness for your arrival. Or is that a fantasy? In any event, you were once again starting from scratch, gathering your brood and launching a whole new life. You had lots of hands and feet to pitch in with the tangible workload, but there's no doubt in my mind that you were the backbone that guided the family in the right way to live. You all found a place of honour in your new community, and we in the generations to follow are indebted to you for that. Thank you.

I'll be writing again, to chat about your days back in Calgary.

Your loving granddaughter,
Eleanor

Mildred King Snowden
Born April 17, 1899—Preston, Lancashire, England
Died July 10, 1991—Calgary, Alberta, Canada

Dear Aunt Millie,

I've been travelling back to the Great War in my thoughts, and thinking of the King family's involvement, which was extensive. Yes, we had three warriors in your father and your brothers, but in my books, the other four of you were brave warriors, too. So today I'm writing to chat about your experience during those years.

You were sweet sixteen when the family returned to Preston, and suddenly propelled into oldest-child status, a role I know you would have assumed seriously and responsibly. You found work at the military payroll office, your income contributing to the family's welfare on the home front. One of the first things you learned on the job was that, when encountering the letter "V" beside a soldier's name on the payroll, you were to deduct a set amount from his pay. In the absence of an explanation, you just executed orders. I remember you telling me that it was many years before you learned that the "V" stood for venereal disease. I wondered why the soldiers' medical circumstance called for a deduction in pay, but you, with that impish glint in your eye, wondered how those *marked* guys were explaining their pay deduction to their wives.

One thing you dreaded about that job was the walk home after work in winter when blackouts were in effect. You talked about groping your way in the pitch dark, often feeling like you had completely lost your bearings. You'd heave a sigh of relief at the welcoming silhouette of your church, when it made a ghostly appearance, like out of Dickens' *Great*

Expectations. Your route took you through the churchyard, so you knew you were heading in the right direction. Too often, however, you'd lose the direct path through the churchyard and find yourself in the church's graveyard, where relief turned to terror. As if that wasn't frightening enough, a mentally challenged boy, who lived near you on Manchester Road, took great pleasure in sneaking up behind you in the graveyard, and scaring the wits out of you. How brave you were, getting up the next day, and repeating this journey all over again.

I felt for you when you lamented that you felt like a misfit with the local girls, many of whom worked in Preston's cotton mills. You described them as "coarse," their behaviour and language running in opposition to your upbringing. The one place where you found comfort was in your church, which you attended every Sunday. Your favourite story was of spotting an injured soldier in church one Sunday, and, after striking up a conversation, discovered that he was Canadian. That automatically qualified him for an invitation to Sunday dinner and a place in the special visitor's sitting room. Grandma welcomed him with open arms, and you were pretty pleased with the role you played in bringing happiness to a lonely Canadian. In time, however, you were disappointed to learn that all soldiers weren't as honourable as those you'd been exposed to in your home environment.

On Sunday afternoons, your favourite pastime was to visit relatives about five miles away, your route taking you through Avenham Park, which opened into a large open field that had become a favourite hangout for off-duty soldiers. You became the object of their vulgar jeers, which shocked and frightened you. When your relatives learned that one soldier laughingly chased you one day, they insisted you come by train for all future visits. You agreed, though reluctantly, because you much preferred to walk.

You were a big help to your mother with the cooking, and, much to her relief, I'm sure, you welcomed every opportunity to do the shopping for supplies. You learned that the best deals for food were in the open market, so you shopped there exclusively. You never forgot the merchant who wouldn't allow you to touch the produce or make a purchase until 11 a.m. His restrictions were a puzzle and an annoyance. Then one day you learned that his bewildering habit was actually a clever ruse—by making customers wait, it led them to believe that his goods were special, better than anything offered by the competition. You didn't take kindly to this underhanded tactic, so you made a conscious decision to let him know that—you took all your business to the competitor.

I smile at this story, Aunt Millie. I knew you as Dad's partner in the restaurant business, and I know that no one ever pulled the wool over your eyes when you were in that capacity either. I also know how invaluable you were to the success of the business. But that's for another day. It's been lovely having this chat, and I think we've gotten to know each other even better than before. You are the best!

Much love,
Eleanor

Henry Clement King Jr. (Harry)
Born June 20, 1900—Preston, Lancashire, England
Died January 14, 1947—Calgary, Alberta, Canada

Dear Uncle Harry,

Since I've got the Great War on my brain, I'd like to chat with you about your boyhood back in Preston during the war years. You were a lad of fifteen when you returned to Preston during the war, and overnight you had become the new man of the house. I'm only just realizing how little I know about your life during those years, so I find myself filling in the blanks by summation. I trust your mother enrolled you in school somewhere, perhaps night school, which I know Dad attended, although family talk about you never seemed to focus on school, but rather your job working at *Lingards*, the tony menswear store in the core of Preston. I believe *Lingards* was owned by a relative of your mother's. Just imagine, you were attending to suit fittings for Preston's establishment when you were scarcely out of breeks yourself. You had to grow up fast, didn't you? I'll bet you were an authority on the latest fashion trends in no time. Yet in spite of all you achieved at such a tender age, the favourite story that your thankless family carried home to Canada with them—the story they laughingly repeated many times over—centred on your legendary absentmindedness. You know what's coming, don't you? Since no one is better at self-deprecating humour than the Kings, I know you'll bear with yet another telling of the family's favourite story:

On this particular day, you walked home from work as always, dressed smartly in your tweed *Lingards* sports jacket, with the family's newspaper tucked under your arm. It had grown dark, and with blackouts in effect, dark was dark. You sauntered through the front door of the property four doors from the corner, in the terraced setting where you lived and where all the front doors looked alike. Tired after a long day on your feet, you tossed your umbrella into the stand, kicked off your shoes, and made yourself at home. I'm not sure who was more surprised, you or the homeowner, when he encountered a stranger in his parlour, feet up, nose buried in a newspaper. From that day forward, you counted the doors from the corner: one, two, *three*. Yes, the third door, not the fourth. Are you aware that we tease your son Ritchie about being absentminded? Even he will agree that it's justified. So much for my theory that traits skip a generation—that one travelled direct.

I can count on there being a lot more stories about you during those years, but it looks like you're in luck—they never made it this far. So I guess that will be it for now. But I promise I'll write again.

Lots of love,
Eleanor

Horace — My Father

Dear Dad,

I have been writing to your family about their experiences during the Great War, and I'm writing to you last. (The youngest is always the last, right?) You were just fourteen years old when you landed back in Preston. Even though it was your hometown, it would have been totally unfamiliar, because you last saw it when you were a child of three. You were also contending with a war raging close by, and the uneasy knowledge that your father and two big brothers were daily risking their lives in it. I remember fourteen as an age when my friends and the security of my home were the two most critical things in the world to me. Here you were, in a strange setting, your friends oceans away and three trusted members of the family were absent from your household. You had no idea for how long, and you lived in constant fear for their safety. These must not have been happy years for you.

I've been trying to piece together your education from family notes, and in particular, some stories that you wrote yourself in your later years. You attended a County Council School for one period, which I assume was a school funded by the state. However, you wanted to contribute to the family income, so you went to work for Thomas Robinson, food administrator at the Preston Town Hall, while continuing your education at night school. I had forgotten that your first encounter with the food industry was at such a young age.

Night school took place at the Harris Institute for veterans and their dependents, the student population largely made up of veterans, who were much older than you. You were impressed with the dedication of these *mature* students, who were keen to learn, and were grateful for the opportunity. One veteran, who befriended you, was a guy who had lost an arm in combat, and he now wore a wooden prosthesis. You welcomed his friendship, but he had an annoying habit of smacking your elbow with his wooden arm. Teenage guys never want to reveal weakness, so you put up with his painful teasing, but you never forgot how much it hurt!

The only civilian student in your class, beside you, was Jim, and the two of you became best friends. Your favourite extracurricular activity was riding your bikes in Avenham Park, where bikes were prohibited. You rascals relished encounters with the park policeman who, confined to walking the beat, was powerless to stop your speeding bikes. He would raise his arms commanding you to stop, but, cheeky pair that you were, you'd sail on by, laughing your heads off at the poor man flailing in futility. Then one day, you were speeding down the steep hill at the park entrance as usual, and looked up to see four burly policemen standing directly in your path, with outstretched arms firmly linked. You had seconds to make a decision—do we surrender or go for it? You and Jim glanced at one another, and in silent communication, recognized the bobbies' dilemma—break their holds or risk getting their arms broken. Already in full downhill propulsion, you nodded in agreement, lowered your heads, and went for it. At the last moment, the bobbies released their grips, and stood back, fearing for their lives. You and Jim didn't stop laughing for the rest of the day. But it was a shallow victory—you never risked riding your bikes in Avenham Park again. The eye-opening follow-up to the story is that the two of you ultimately matured beyond your years, most notably in one surprising way.

As you sat through evening classes together, unfamiliar language from the mouths of the veterans kept assaulting your senses—casual, repugnant profanity. You, especially, had never been exposed to such language in your own home, yet it appeared to be the standard battlefield lingo of the soldier. You personally wanted to avoid such language from slipping into your own vocabulary, so you made a firm commitment to yourself to never swear. Further to that, you asked your friend Jim if he'd agree to make a pledge with you. Jim agreed, and the two of you turned deaf ears to the night school profanities, and held firm to your commitments.

A couple of years later, Jim was called into the army, and when he came home on leave, he couldn't wait to see you. Likewise, you were excited to see your best friend after such a long separation. But the joy of the reunion was dashed—Jim was swearing like a trooper. I know that story saddened you, Dad, but never mind, you remained resolute ... for life. I never heard you swear. Not once.

You were sixteen years old when the war ended. You had lost your big brother, your dad was not well, and your schooling was in disarray, but you were becoming proficient in the school of life. You had carved out some principles for yourself, gained knowledge in the business world, learned how to type, dabbled in the intricacies of watchmaking, and experienced grief. By the time you landed back in Canada, you were seventeen years old, and although you lacked the formal education afforded most guys your age, you were blessed with many advantages—native intelligence, good instincts, and an abundance of energy and drive—all the qualities you needed to establish yourself successfully in your new community of Calgary. And that's what you did.

There's so many things I want to reminisce about, surrounding your early Calgary days, but I'd better save it for another time ... the list is long. Sure missing you, Dad.

Till next time ... .
Lots of love,
El

—Chapter Three—
Civilian Heroes

The Andersons

Dear Grandpa,

So there you were in Calgary, a young and promising city, if only it weren't so far from home. The 1,800-mile separation from family must have felt almost insurmountable. You were as alone as you'd ever been, without a roof over your head, no job prospect in sight, and the responsibility for your family weighing heavily on your shoulders. All this, when you'd scarcely had time to regain your strength, following your lengthy confinement in a sanatorium battling tuberculosis. Describing it as a truly a life-altering illness was not an understatement. It was May 1907, and the chill in the air was dampening your spirits even further.

Your mindset was to faithfully comply with your doctor's foremost order—to "find outdoor work in Alberta's dry air," which certainly limited options for employment. Regrettably, your previous experience as a telegrapher fell outside the prescribed orders. You had been a skilled telegrapher, had loved your work, and it had provided a comfortable living for you. Now you had to give it up. But you were resourceful, and you very quickly found a solution—you became a conductor on the Calgary streetcar, a system of transportation that was in its infancy in the city. This work did not offer you the status that you had previously enjoyed, nor did it provide a comparable income, but it did give you the comfort of knowing you were doing the right thing for your health and your future well-being. And you know, Grandpa, I have a happy vision of you engaged in that job. Mother always described you as fun-loving, with a good sense of humour. I see you brightening the day for yawning passengers as they boarded your streetcar for their morning commute, and, likewise, you would have lifted the spirits of those boarding at end of day, tired, and maybe out-of-sorts.

The scene in my mind's eye that I love best, is of Grandmother arriving in Calgary by train, with Ruby and Lillian in tow. You were a family again! Such excitement. I can picture little Ruby—my mother—busying about to help her mother set up housekeeping in the rental home that you had secured at 216 - 4th Avenue West. Do you think she had any concept of the permanence of this move? Any idea that she would seldom see her beloved aunt and uncle and cousins in Ottawa again? I know that Maria understood it all too well. Meanwhile, there was lots to distract everyone. You had scouted the surrounding area, and made plans to take your family on a walkabout, to visit the school and the church that would play important roles in the lives of your girls. And so, life in Calgary began.

I have conjured a vision of your household, from descriptions that Mother and Aunt Lil passed on to me through the years. The first descriptor that comes to mind is *peaceful*—I see four calm people living in harmony. Am I right? Then I would use the words *mannerly* and *polite*, because Mother was a stickler for manners, which I assume she learned as a child at your table. I have a clear picture of the four of you observing table etiquette— please pass the bread (no reaching), use the butter knife, don't talk with your mouth full, elbows off the table, and ask to be excused before leaving the table. I know all this, Grandpa, because that's how it was for me growing up.

Grandmother would have kept an orderly house, clean and tidy, and you could count on freshly ironed shirts every day and a hot meal on the table promptly at 6:00 o'clock. There's comfort in this vision, although I sort of sense that you might have enjoyed a little disorderliness now and then. Maybe less perfect and more fun, what do you think? And tell me if I'm right—I see Ruby leaning toward her mother's restrained bearing, while Lillian was more of a free spirit. Their childhood photos draw hints of my theory, with Mother wearing the look of the serious, responsible big sister, and Aunt Lil, with a glint in her eye, looking ready to break loose, given the chance. As young women, however, life got serious for both of them, didn't it?

Grandmother developed an unsightly lesion on her face, which was eventually diagnosed as malignant, a frightening thing for all of you, but especially for her. It grew rapidly, soon threatening her life. Poor dear, would have longed to have her sister with her at such a time. Mother said you did all in your power to save her, including borrowing a hundred dollars from your brother Clayton to take her to the Mayo Clinic in Rochester, New York. Weren't you surprised, when the Mayo Clinic assured you that Calgary's own McGuffin Clinic could manage her case as effectively as they—or anyone else—could? And so you returned home, and arranged for radiation treatments with Dr. McGuffin. Sadly, he was unable to contain the spread, and the disease ate away more and more of her beautiful face. By this time, Mother was attending Normal School, and dropped out to care for her mother full time. And I know for a fact, Grandpa, that she never felt duty-bound to do this. In spite of the heartache and fatigue that she experienced tending to her mother, she considered it a privilege to be the one at her bedside. She loved her dearly, and always teared up when telling me about her final days. Grandmother died the day before Mother's Day, with her devoted nursemaid holding her hand.

    I trust your girls kept the household running for you after your Maria died, and I know that when Mother and Dad married in 1927, you, and, briefly, Lillian, were welcomed into their first house at 739 - 12th Avenue West. Do you have any idea how envious I am of my big brother Stan, who got to have you for the first eight years of his life? He always talked about you teaching him Morse Code and launching him on his first two-wheeler. He remembers you holding onto the seat of his bike and running him up and down the sidewalk on 7th street, until he got the hang of it. Evidently he was a slow learner, so you got quite a workout. I was denied happy memories such as Stan enjoyed, but I do have an item of yours that once sat in his bedroom, before making its way to me. Your small, oak flip-down desk—with the scroll enhancement on the front—keeps your memory alive for me. I picture you sitting at this desk to write letters, maybe to your brother Clayt. Thoughts of letter-writing always make me happy.

Till next time … .
Much love,
Eleanor

Dear Grandmother,

Moving from Montreal to Calgary doesn't seem like such a big deal today, considering we can fly that distance in four hours, and communicate with family members through the magic of *cyberspace* with *smart phones* and *computers* in seconds. (I'm going to have to save a fuller explanation of all this for another time.) But don't think for a minute that I've ever downplayed what a major move it was for you and your girls in 1907. Ruby was just four and a half and Lillian, a one-year-old. The separation from family members back east, especially Sadie and Clayton, would have felt monumental to you. It's understandable that your loneliness became so profound that, two years later, you and the girls travelled back to Ottawa, for one more embrace from your beloved sister, Sadie. It was a treasured time that raised your spirits and helped you come to terms with your new life out west. Even so, I'm sure your second parting was agonizing. It breaks my heart to know that you saw Sadie only one more time after that.

Sadie came west with her children, Marge and Earle, for a summer visit in 1914. Mother was then a child of twelve, and I have to tell you, she talked about that special time for the rest of her days. She loved being with her *double* cousins, and was especially enamoured by Earle, who found no end of ways to entertain her with mischievous antics. She was sure that you and Sadie didn't know about the string he ran from the upstairs window of the boarder's room down to the backyard, which he snapped in the middle of the night, scaring poor Mr. Dickens half to death. But I know that mothers have eyes in the back of their heads, and I'm guessing that you turned your back on some of his boyish mischief, smiling to yourself as you allowed his antics to intrude on the proper lives of your girls. (I can see Grandpa laughing his head off at Earle scaring the daylights out of Mr. Dickens.) Cousin Marge, from all descriptions, was a polar opposite to her rascally little brother—dignified, fashionable, beautifully coiffed, a perfect lady. Mother idolized her. But Earle was more fun.

I don't need to tell you that Mother was a sensitive child, and more than anyone, I think she understood your loneliness living in Calgary. Witnessing your joy at being with Sadie in the summer of '14 touched her deeply. But in spite of an underlying sadness, you never let your family down. You watched over Grandpa's health, maintained a warm, safe haven for your family, and took in a boarder to supplement income. Your sewing skills were also a huge asset, as you took in projects for friends and neighbours, while keeping yourself and your girls beautifully dressed with your Singer sewing machine.

I have found the Anderson addresses in Calgary's old directories, and I see that the family moved six times between your arrival in 1907 and 1927, the year my parents married. That's a lot of packing and unpacking. You might be interested to know that, for some unexplained reason, only one address held any significance for Mother—216 - 4th Avenue West, where she lived from age six to age thirteen. All her memories seemed to flow from that home; it must have been a happy, carefree time in her life. When I was a child, we often took a Sunday drive, and Dad was programmed to include this particular home on our route. I have to confess that, to me, that house looked like a cold, dreary barn with its drab, weathered exterior and barn-shaped roof. I never told Mother that, though, because it was abundantly evident that she didn't see barn—or cold. She saw warmth and happiness. At one time, perhaps in the '70s, there was a rumour that the new owner of that property, who had purchased it for his car dealership, intended to move the house to our now burgeoning Heritage Park. Great excitement turned to disappointment when this did not come to fruition. Alas, it was demolished instead.

Life would not have been easy for you or Grandpa, but I hope you know that you raised two girls who grew up with memories of a happy childhood. Mother talked about learning to skate by pushing a little red chair around the rink that Grandpa flooded in the backyard, and learning to swim in the Cave and Basin pool in Banff. She rarely participated in any of our recreational pursuits when I was a kid, but I have fond memories of her in speed skates, gliding arm in arm with Dad in perfect sync across our community rink. And I see her gliding one other place—in the Cave and Basin pool when we holidayed in Banff. Always sidestroke, in her green-skirted bathing suit. Once at the Cave's warm pool, when she and I had changed into our clothes after swimming, I ran to the edge of the pool, calling to my dad and my brothers that it was time to leave. I was very little—no more than three years old, I'm guessing—and I slipped off the edge of the pool, falling in face first. I've never forgotten the sensation of whirling like a windmill beneath the surface, before a hand suddenly plucked me out. Dad and the boys were nearby in the pool, but Mother hadn't waited for them, or anyone else. She had stepped fully clothed into the pool to fish me out. No wonder I always felt safe with my mom.

Mother and Aunt Lil spoke fondly of their school days—their nine years at *Central Public School* and then *Calgary Collegiate Institute* for high school. Since they lived in Calgary during its earliest days, they developed quite an appreciation for its history, especially the history of their schools. I followed them into the same high school, and Mother and I even attended a school reunion together once. She was scarcely through the door when she spotted one of her teachers. It took me two hours to find one of mine. And I especially loved watching Mother taking in the Stampede Parade every year. When the *old-timers'* car came by, she could name everyone in it.

You know, of course, that your girls excelled in school, and both went on to Normal School, where they achieved teaching certificates. You also know that Mother dropped out of Normal School for a term to spend your final days at your bedside. She'd want you to know that she did return to earn her teaching certificate. In the end, by her own admission, she never particularly liked formal teaching, and chose to be a full-time homemaker, which she was very good at. And, let me tell you, she excelled at teaching on the home front—correct grammar, proper manners, consideration for others, and the dictates of an unwavering moral code. Sometimes I think that some of these admirable elements are getting neglected in home schooling today. Aunt Lil was a gifted kindergarten and Grade 1 teacher for many years. You can rest assured that she included all the above dictates in her classrooms, along with the ABCs.

Well, Grandmother, I'll always regret that fate never allowed us to meet, yet I believe your loving spirit made its presence known through my mother. And, more tangibly, you might like to know that I have a couple of items of yours that Mother treasured and passed down to me—a gilt-edged serving dish with a lid, and an Oriental-looking tea set—teapot, sugar bowl, and two cups and saucers. You might think that I'm foolish, but I don't use these rather delicate items, for fear they'll get broken in our household of rambunctious grandchildren. So they grace the display shelves in our family room, where I can glance up and say, "Good morning, Grandmother, nice to have you with me today."

I love you!
Eleanor

Dear Mother,

Your carefree life as a child in Montreal, with doting parents and a new baby sister, was turned upside down when your father contracted tuberculosis, wasn't it? Especially when he had to leave his three ladies behind to enter a sanatorium. I have been patching together a story of your early days, through the compact messages on your extensive postcard collection. I smile when I see the one-cent stamps on the cards—a penny for your thoughts! A penny doesn't even exist in our currency anymore. But your card collection still exists, thanks to Don, who guarded it with his life, and now it's in my safekeeping.

The cards give me a glimpse into the movement of your family during the unsettling period when your father was isolated from you, and later when he travelled west to scope out a new life. Some cards tell me very little: "Hope you are having a pleasant summer." And some say nothing at all; I suppose the sender presumed that just finding a surprise in your mailbox was excitement enough. I'll confess that one such wordless, unsigned postcard addressed to you in your father's unmistakable handwriting, saddened me. Granted you were only four years old and could not yet read, and he was in isolation in Ste. Agathe, but I nevertheless ached to see at least two simple words: "Love, Daddy." But then, you knew that he loved you.

One of your most faithful correspondents was your beloved Aunt Carrie, second wife of Will, your father's oldest brother. Throughout ages four and five, you received a whole string of *Roosevelt Bears* postcards from Aunt Carrie, cleverly designed cards from the children's book series, *The Roosevelt Bears,* by Seymour Eaton. By the way, do you know how the designation *Teddy* of teddy bears originated? It began with a story involving US President Theodore (Teddy) Roosevelt in 1902, coincidentally the year of your birth. The president and some of his friends were on a hunting trip on the Mississippi, and after several hours without success, they suddenly came upon a bear. Quickly surrounding it, Roosevelt's friends urged him to shoot it for trophy. But the president refused to shoot the helpless animal, and his show of mercy quickly became headline news across the country. Shortly thereafter, a Brooklyn storeowner decided to make toy bears for his shop, and asked Roosevelt for permission to name his cuddly toy *Teddy*. And that's how the teddy bear was born. Books and cards followed. Seymour Eaton began writing a series of books, in which he now capitalized on Roosevelt's surname. The *Roosevelt Bears* became the most popular children's books in America at the time, and postcards featuring illustrations from the books became a sought-after sideline. Assuming your cards might now be popular amongst collectors, I researched duplicates of Aunt Carrie's cards to you.

Guess what? Collectors are paying upwards of $200.00 for some of them. But it goes without saying—Aunt Carrie's *Roosevelt Bears* are priceless.

The summer of '07 brought despair and joy wrapped in the same parcel—the sadness of separation from your father, who had travelled alone to Calgary, and the excitement of bunking in for the summer with your beloved Ottawa family—Aunt Sadie, Uncle Clayton, and double cousins, Marge and Earle. Aunt Carrie, residing in Banff at the time, assigned herself the job of go-between, sending cards and news to your lonely dad in Calgary, and to the rest of you in Ottawa. Between the lines, her anxiety was evident—she couldn't hide her concern over the upheaval taking place within the family.

No. 8. The Roosevelt Bears at the Tailor's.
"Two tailors came with cloth and tape
To fit them out in handsome shape."

Her September 18, 1907, card was unlike all others, with its unusual photograph of forty-two toddler-sized orphans in a French crèche. Was it a random selection, or did she have some connection to this crèche? Was it perhaps a favourite charity, because she did not have children of her own? In any event, I'm sure you've already guessed what made that card special—yes, it was the first one addressed to you in Calgary, signalling that your family was at last together again. The full message was four words: "Welcome to the West." I can imagine the joyful reunion with your dad, but

I'm also mindful that you were already missing your beloved Ottawa cousins.

Aunt Carrie's *Roosevelt Bears* cards continued to arrive, but now interspersed among them, two collectible cards appear from London, England's famous *Tuck's Post Cards*. These cards fascinate me, so I've done a little research on them. They were processed in Bavaria, and referred to as *oilettes*, their style giving them the look of an oil painting. My research further reveals that the two particular cards of yours, entitled *Go It Dinah* and *Sweet Hearts*, are from a series of only six cards, depicting darling little black children at play. I don't know how to say this, except that the title of that series of cards would now be considered a cringe-worthy racial slur. Dear, benevolent Aunt Carrie would roll in her grave if she knew that, a century after she lovingly selected two *Happy Little Coons* cards for her sweet, innocent niece, the world would gasp in horror. We know that Aunt Carrie had only love in her heart.

You also received cards from a little friend named Gay, who was evidently on extended travels with her family. The thing about Gay's cards that especially bring a smile to my face, is how they were addressed—Miss Ruby Anderson, 4th Avenue West, Calgary. In the absence of your house number, Gay's mother had carefully written a critical piece of information along the bottom of each card: "Opposite Braemar Lodge." They always found you, didn't they? Everyone in town knew Braemar Lodge.

Cards flowed from everywhere. The eastern family, in Ottawa, wrote regularly, from the standard message, "Missing you and hope you are well," to specific thank-you notes, "Thank you for the pretty hair ribbons, Auntie." I picture young Marge, ribbons trailing from her flowing locks, dancing with delight at the gift from her beloved Aunt Maria. Young Marge's cards were newsier than Carrie's, but no cards topped Aunt Carrie's for classiness or sheer volume.

I remember you telling me the terrible story of your Uncle Will—your mother's brother—being killed on a railway track. The manual handcar that he was operating had been struck by a train. His family was clearly reluctant to share the details of his grim demise with your mother, until May—Will's daughter—sent a postcard in August 1912. It informed the family that a friend travelling to Calgary, would be arriving with a letter of introduction. "She will be able to tell you of our 'trouble,'" May explained, "as she was with us nearly all the time, and knows the particulars." That card paints a whole picture for me—poor May could only face her father's harrowing death by referring to it as "trouble," while assigning an explanation of "the particulars" to her friend, who was a complete stranger to her Aunt Maria. How I weep for your mother. I'm guessing she enjoyed little communication with her brother, Will, and suddenly he was lost to her forever. Did you even know your Uncle Will?

A few messages also arrived from neighbours, each conjuring up a story in a handful of words, such as the neighbours travelling to Chicago, having deposited their cats in your family's care: "Hope the cats are alive and not bothering you too much." I can see cats upsetting your mother's perfect house, but I know that you and Aunt Lil both loved cats, so you would have been a happy pair. Others travelling farther afield sent exotic cards, with undreamed-of news from an unknown world. "Returning from pilgrimage to Mecca," one writer said. "I'm writing this message while the caravan is resting." Such travel would have been incomprehensible to your family. I think of brother Don when I read your 1911 card from England— "We are still in London. Saw the Coronation of King George V today." Don would have been beside himself knowing someone who had actually attended a coronation. George V and Queen Mary grace the front of this card, with the names of the five British possessions arching above their heads: Canada, India, Britannia, Australasia, S. Africa. And across the bottom of the card, the words of Tennyson read: *God Save our King and Queen. One with Britain, heart and soul! One life, one flag, one fleet, one Throne!"*

For some years, you had a boarder, Mr. Dickens, living with the family to help augment the income. When I was a child, you frequently talked about him, always with affection, but always formally—"*Mr.* Dickens." I always wondered what his first name was. Just curious. When he sailed to England in the spring of 1912 on the trip of a lifetime, he sent postcards to each member of the family. When I came across Mr. Dickens's cards, I thought, aha, now I'll learn his first name ... until I read the salutation on your father's card: "Dear Anderson..." and the unrevealing complimentary closing: "Sincerely, Dickens." So Mr. Dickens still had no first name.

To you, a child of ten at the time, Mr. Dickens wrote kind words: "Dear Ruby, Have not forgotten you and shall be glad to see you again." But I'm especially drawn to the front of the card postmarked May 4, 1912, containing the photo of an all-too-familiar ship. Its caption read: THE ILL-FATED AMERICAN LINER "TITANIC." The liner had gone down a scant two weeks prior, yet this postcard was already in circulation. Stranger yet, it was described as an *American* liner, when it actually belonged to the White Star Line, a British fleet. Stranger still, Mr. Dickens did not breathe a word of The Titanic's sinking in his message. Back home, you had learned all about the ship's disaster, and had been living in fear that your friend may have been onboard. His card brought you welcome relief—he was alive and dry.

Interestingly, after unearthing the error on the Titanic card, I came across another, in a letter written to me by Aunt Lil. While describing your childhood together, she told the story of the bouquet of garden flowers that the two of you assembled and donated to an auction in aid of the war effort. The best part of the story was that Mr. R. B. Bennett, your future prime minister, bought your flowers and personally wrote you a note: "I bought your bouquet. Thank you. May you live long to help your King." Trusting Aunt Lil's airtight memory, I inserted her story into my book, *The House With The Light On*. Well, guess what? While thumbing through your postcards, I came across one with a photo of King George V on the front, and the message, penned in a rather childlike scrawl, brought a smile to my face. The card, dated September, 1914, is addressed to Miss Ruby Anderson (perhaps Lillian received a separate card). It read: "Dear Friend, Having bought the beautiful bouquet made by you for Patriotic Fund, I hope you may live long to serve your King. I am your friend, J.A. McArthur M.P.P. Gleichen." You and Aunt Lil would not have known the M.P.P. from Gleichen, but you did know R. B. Bennett, the VIP who happened to be your next-door neighbour. It makes perfect sense to me that Lillian's imagination, at age eight, simply supplanted the political figure unfamiliar to her with the one she knew by sight—her neighbour. And that's the image—and the story—that stayed with her forever after.

So ... after two years in Calgary, in which I know your mother would have been heartsick with loneliness, I find myself palpating with excitement knowing that she boarded the train back to Ottawa, with you and Lillian. The excitement of that reunion with your Ottawa family must have been beyond imagining. You were not yet seven years old, but I remember you talking about it to your dying day. And once again, postcards enhance the story.

On September 18, 1909, your mother gives me a glimpse into the joyous time in a card to your dad, written as the three of you were about to embark on the short train ride from Ottawa to Montreal to visit Aunt Carrie and Uncle Will: "We are leaving this afternoon for Montreal. Just read your letter this morning. Glad to know you are getting along all right. We are all fine. The children are having a lovely time. MA." I'm intrigued with her closing—just her initials, "*MA.*" Do you think she would have considered any display of affection on a postcard to be improper? That aside, this card has special meaning for me, for one main reason—it's the only sample I have of Grandmother Anderson's handwriting. And I have to say, her script isn't what I would describe as elegant. It definitely doesn't suggest the grace that she was known to carry.

Your dad received one other postcard from Ottawa while you were on that visit. It comically refuted your mother's words of assurance, that you were "all fine." No hiding the truth for Cousin Marge—she picked up her pen and spilled the beans: "Dear Uncle Rube, I thought I would write and tell you Ruby has the chickenpox. She is not very sick, but is covered all over... ." Her card had me laughing out loud. Finally, it was Aunt Carrie who told me when the happy reunion with your cousins was coming to an end. Her October 6 card, sent to you as you were preparing to leave Ottawa for home, said, "Good bye, Dear Ruby. Hope to see you again before long." Tears must have flowed on the train ride back to Calgary. I always sensed that your mother never stopped longing for her life in the East, and often, I wondered whether that loneliness did not spill over into your psyche. What do you think?

When you were settled back in Calgary once and for all, it was time to start school. You enrolled at *Central Public School*, and they were happy years for you. You loved school, excelled academically, and you and your little sister were surrounded by a new circle of friends. Your father was regaining his health, and your mother was finding stability and joy in her family, her home, and her church. Life was good. It was no doubt insignificant to you at the time, but you were a very early student in a very historic school, which opened in 1905. And I'll bet you didn't know that your next-door neighbour and member of parliament, R. B. Bennett (the man who didn't purchase your flowers), spoke at the ribbon-cutting of your school. He didn't mince words when he directed sage advice to the young male students of the day: "*No boy is a better man or better able to make his way in the world because he could swear or smoke a cigarette.*" How many guys took notice of his words, do you think?

You attended that school from grades one to nine, and then enrolled in the *Calgary Collegiate Institute* (CCI) for high school. It became *Central High School* by the time I went there, although even then it never seemed certain of its correct designation. One of my yearbooks, *The Analecta*, has *CCI* splashed across the front cover, *Central High School* down its spine, and on the title page inside, *Central Collegiate Institute*, a designation it never owned in its life. Our principal, listed in the *Analecta* as its business advisor, either wasn't paying attention, or couldn't make up his mind who we were. *Central High* closed as a high school in 1965, but has served in an educational capacity ever since. It is now designated a heritage site; its preserved sandstone facade peeks out from behind a new ten-storey building housing offices of the Calgary Board of Education Centre.

Meanwhile, in 1939, your *Central Public School* was reorganized as a Junior High School only, and renamed *James Short Junior High School* in honour of a former principal. Thirty years later it was forced to close due to diminishing enrolment. Soon after that, it was demolished. But its landmark cupola survived to keep the school's memory alive. For some years, this cupola struck a pose from a place of honour in *James Short Park* on the corner of Centre

Street and 4th Avenue Southwest, where it was frequently photographed with Calgary's imposing skyscraper, *The Bow*, as a backdrop. Then one day, Calgarians became aware that, in fact, the renowned James Short had displayed racist tendencies when it came to his relationship with our Asian community. And so, in 2022, the park was renamed *Harmony Park*. Good heavens, I hadn't intended to give you a history lesson. But I do know that you'd enjoy knowing the final chapters of your schools.

Well, Mother, I hope you've enjoyed reliving your childhood with me. I'll save the later years for another letter. Now, I think it would be fitting to let your beloved Aunt Carrie close this letter with her beautiful little greeting card, dated Tuesday, October 12, 1937. You know the one—with the padded, satin-embossed cover. It reads, "*Congratulations, and Welcome to the New Little Girl.*" Aunt Carrie's familiar handwriting appears on the back: "My Dear Ruby, I am so pleased to hear from Lillian, the news of wee Eleanor Ruby's safe arrival. She already has her place in my heart, as you all have. My love and congratulations, Aunt Carrie." I never met Aunt Carrie, but she will always have a place in my heart … alongside you!

Much love,
Eleanor
xxxOOO

Sarah Lillian Whitney Anderson King

Born April 11, 1906, Montreal, Quebec, Canada
Died September 2, 2000, White Rock, BC, Canada

Dear Aunt Lil,

I'll never forget that September day we lost you. My gang was at our cabin celebrating grandson Andrew's fifth birthday, when Rich phoned with the news of your unexpected death in White Rock. Such a coincidence that our little birthday boy was poised to begin kindergarten, on the very day that you, super kindergarten teacher, left us. I was not ready.

I am comforted to know that you and Mother had happy childhoods, given the fact that you both met with challenges in adulthood. Even so, I always think of you as a happy person. You met your challenges with a smile. I don't need to remind you how special you were to me. Being Mother's sister married to Dad's brother and living just down the street qualified you as my second mother. Later in life you earned a new distinction—you became my loyal penpal. Our correspondence began when you retired from teaching Grade 1 with the Calgary School Board, the board having turned down your request to continue teaching past its mandatory retirement age of sixty-five. We all knew that you had so much more to offer, but rules were rules. So you took your much-more-to-offer off to the International School in Dar es Salaam, Tanzania, East Africa, where your son, Rich, and his wife, Mavis, were living and working. Your letters from Tanzania during your two years there were publication-worthy ... as were your chronicles the world over, as you globe-trotted for the rest of your life. You chose White Rock, BC, for your retirement, where you tastefully decorated a charming apartment to be your safe haven between travels.

We wrote continuously, until you said a final goodbye at age ninety-four. I sometimes think that, if the pages of our combined letters were laid out end to end, they'd reach from Calgary to White Rock. What do you think? For a long time after you were gone, I grieved every time I lifted the lid on my mailbox, knowing there was not going to be a letter from you to brighten my day.

I have to confess, Aunt Lil, that I always sort of took you for granted, because I saw a woman managing life so successfully. The fact is, you lost your mother when you were eighteen years old, an age when a young woman needs her mother's understanding and counsel. Then at the age of forty, you faced widowhood with three young children to raise. Whew! I now know that it could not have been easy—you just made it look easy.

Well, Aunt Lil, guess where my letter-writing is taking me now? I've been writing all my grandparents, trying to get to know them, since they left this life before I arrived. Remember when I wrote you years ago, asking about the personalities of your parents? You replied by return mail, as I expected you would. Good news! I just found that letter in my keeper box, and when I read it the second time, I laughed all over again. You enclosed a quote that you believed was made by Mark Twain's daughter: "Mother likes morals. Dad likes cats." It's not only comical, it's telling. I always believed that Grandmother was warm and loving, but uncomfortably strait-laced. Grandpa, on the other hand, wanted to let loose now and then, and have some fun. Further, you suggested that you didn't think theirs was a particularly happy marriage, but rather one of convenience. The only time you saw them demonstrate affection was at Christmas one year—they put on a record and danced! You and Mother were ecstatic.

Christmas was a serious religious celebration for your mother, whereas your dad saw it as a Santa Claus, hang-up-the-stockings occasion. Your mother, a staunch Methodist, went to church twice every Sunday year round. Your father never attended ... until she died. Then forever after, he never missed. And you never saw your father cry until the moment your mother died, when he burst into tears. Your stories brought them into focus for me. Thank you!

You might be surprised to know that my writing over the past thirty-plus years hasn't been confined to letters. Since we last chatted on paper, I have written three books, and this letter to you will be inserted into my fourth. But I'm telling you this as a segue into a story you won't believe. A group of women, residing in our old neighbourhood, had established a book club, and called me one day with an invitation to be their guest at their Christmas meeting. The organizer kindly offered to pick me up, if I was concerned about night driving or finding my way to the address in the dark of December. The address she gave me—are you ready for this?—was 420 Scarboro Avenue! Your old house! What are the chances? I assured her that I could find my way ... while resisting to add, "in my sleep." So here's how it went:

Climbing your front steps felt like coming home ... until the front door opened. It wasn't your familiar face beaming from inside, nor was the grandfather clock beckoning from its place directly ahead at the end of the hall. Gone, too, were your beautiful antique furnishings (always looking like they'd just been freshly polished), the exquisite Dresden figurines on the mantlepiece, and the piano from its place of honour, in the alcove off the dining room. The truth is, the house was looking a little down in the heels. But I know you would want me to find an upside to the evening, and so, I did. The owner of that beautiful home that you and Uncle Harry built was a happy person—like you—and she absolutely loved her home and her neighbourhood. And her book club of fabulous women surrounded me with untold enthusiasm and warmth.

After Rich called to break the news that you had died, I wasn't surprised to learn that you had managed your death as efficiently as you had managed your life. Recognizing that the end was near, you had placed an envelope on your dresser—addressed to your children—containing pertinent information for settling your affairs. It included your wishes for a celebration service. These instructions ended with a suggestion that, "El might like to say a few words. Maybe two minutes." I agreed, with the full understanding that when you said two minutes you meant two minutes—no waxing on with endless embarrassing praise. Which meant I had to write a succinct reflection. The writing part was easy for me,

Aunt Lil. I simply used your letters to tell your story in your own words. The hard part was the two minutes. You're just going to have to forgive me—I could not do you in two. It took me three.

Love, as always,
El

The Post-War Kings

Dear Grandpa,

The summer of 1919 brought joy, though tinged with sorrow. You were back in Canada, optimistically looking forward to new adventures in a new city. The war was behind you at last ... except was it? Or did its horrors travel home with you, and stalk you forever after? Further, I wonder about your health, knowing that you suffered through numerous bouts of bronchitis, fought for your life against the deadly 1918 'flu, and lost your son on the fields of France. It's a miracle to me that you were still standing. But as I've been getting to know you, I feel certain that you were not just standing at the end, you were standing tall, having served "King and country."

Now here's my next question: With the Kings arriving back in Canada in stages, how did you maintain contact with one another? Today, everyone has a *smart phone* that we carry around in our pockets, a device that allows us to communicate with one another through airwaves. These pocket-sized wonders didn't exist back then, yet you somehow managed to find each other and move forward with plans. Your main plan, established before the war's interruption, was to make Calgary your destination. And so, Walter, the first to arrive, accepted responsibility for hopping a train west to seek out living quarters for the rest of you. The home he found at 812 - 3rd Avenue West became your first Calgary address.

Once again you set up shop, opening a jewellery business at 402 - 6th Street West, moving to 702a - 4th Street West a year later, where you added antiques to your inventory. I understand, however, that Grandma was the impetus behind the antiques. She had studied extensively on the subject during her war years in Preston and had become quite an authority. And good for you, Grandpa—you had the good sense to support her new enterprise. Meanwhile, your children were beginning to make career choices of their own.

Walter and Harry had settled into teaching careers, Millie was a natural clerking at F. E. Osborne's bookstore, and Horace was apprenticing as a watchmaker under you. Within two years, Grandma's antique sales had become so lucrative you dispensed with the jewellery side of the business, and purchased property at 220 - 7th Avenue West, where your perfect partnership established the *House of Antiques*. This address also doubled as the family residence. It was an exciting time for all of you, and with your new pursuit taking flight, you travelled to England on a buying trip. That's when our happy story took a tragic turn.

While in an antique shop in Birmingham, England, finalizing a large order for shipment to Calgary, you suffered a sudden fatal stroke. Your Calgary family received the devastating news by wire. Even though hearts were breaking, cool heads prevailed, and the Preston family was summoned to Birmingham. Family members on both sides of the ocean agreed that the wisest solution was the practical one—to entrust your remains and final rites with the Preston family. They willingly accepted the responsibility, and saw you to your final resting place, back in your hometown. I write this part of your story, Grandpa, with a monster-sized lump in my throat. The grief your Calgary family must have experienced from a distance, is beyond imagining. I also agonize over the limited time you were given to enjoy life in the city of your dreams—a scant five years. You were just getting started.

Well, Grandpa, I'll say good-night for now. I think about you a lot. I see you in my dreams ... I'm a little girl sitting on your knee, and you're fastening a pretty necklace from your jewellery store around my neck. You're singing to me ... maybe a selection from one of your Elite Theatre concerts in Wainwright, like "Cheer Up Molly" or "I Love a Lassie." I'm so sad that you never got to be a grandpa, you would have been the best. Except, what am I saying? You are a grandpa, you're *my* grandpa, and you are the best!

Love you!
Eleanor

Dear Grandma,

I can't begin to imagine your frame of mind as you were sailing for Canada after the war, your family travelling in stages. Walter arrived first in April, then Grandpa followed in June, and finally, I believe, the four of you followed some time in July. You left your adored Arthur behind in a lonely grave in France. You were thrilled to be coming home, but you traveled with a hole in your heart.

You had entrusted Walter, your advance man, with finding living quarters in Calgary, and rustling up the basic necessities for your arrival. Knowing Walter as I did, I think he would have had the house pretty functional in time for your arrival, even if the odd item—like an egg beater or a broom—escaped his list. And please tell me he didn't assign you an army cot to sleep on, Grandma.

Passport photo 1919

I picture Millie being a huge help to you, but how were your big boys around the house? It seems to me this was a time when men viewed household tasks as "woman's work." Come to think of it, though, my dad was never averse to rolling up his sleeves in the kitchen, an attitude he must have adopted under your influence. And speaking of ... I know that you influenced your children in all the right ways. You were the backbone of the family—the one everyone turned to for direction and support.

So you dove in as always, put your household in order, then weathered one more move—to 220 - 7th Avenue West, where the family lived permanently, and where you launched the *House of Antiques* from the same address. The *House of*

Antiques quickly became a household name in Calgary, and, years later, 220 - 7th Avenue was like a second home to me. And Grandma, you won't believe how often through the years, I'd be a guest in someone's home, and the beaming hostess would declare, "This dining room table we're sitting at came from your grandmother's antique shop." And inevitably, she'd qualify her pronouncement by adding, "Mrs. King went that extra mile to find it for me; she just seemed to know exactly what I wanted." Always the table under discussion was beautiful. And I could tell that you not only had good taste, but that you knew the secret of succeeding in business.

Which brings me to a story you'll love. It's a convoluted *friend of a friend* story, but I'll try to make it understandable. The daughter of my friend's friend inherited a unique fireplace screen that flips down flat to double as a tea table. But since it did not suit her modern-day tastes, she was preparing to sell it. Her mother, meanwhile, was telling her bridge

club about this special antique item, describing it as hand-carved, rosewood from the mid-1800s. Offhandedly, she mentioned that its original sales slip was still in their possession, signed in the '20s by Mrs. King of the *House of Antiques*. My friend, a member of the bridge club, perked up her ears. "Hold everything!" she exclaimed. 'I'm sure my friend Eleanor is related to that Mrs. King. She might be interested in the piece." You've guessed the rest of the story, Grandma. The circle is complete—the fireplace screen has come home, where it reminds me of you every day.

I wish I could end this letter on that happy note, but there was a heartbreaking sidebar to your story, wasn't there? Grandpa had become an enthusiastic partner in your flourishing antique business, which prompted him to travel to England on a buying trip. What an exciting time for both of you! But the unthinkable happened—he never came back. He suffered a massive stroke in Birmingham. How do you deal with saying goodbye from oceans away, Grandma? Not only that, this was your second loss to take place in a vacuum; you could not be at Arthur's side when he left you either. My dad said that you threw yourself into the antique shop with renewed vigour, which I hope was cathartic for you. Your heart must have raced the day a shipment of goods arrived from Birmingham. You would have felt Grandpa at your side that day, as you unpacked each item. But then, he was at your side every day.

One year later another prospect caught your eye—the restaurant two doors from the antique shop, which the family frequented, came up for sale. Since it was located nearby, and was already enjoying an established clientele, the family wasted no time making a decision. You pooled forces, and the *Tea Kettle Inn* restaurant was born. As a child, I always thought it providence that you chose Millie and Horace to run the restaurant, because I saw what a winning team they were. The truth of the matter was, they were the two who had missed out on secondary educations, which might have pointed them in other directions, so you simply handed the reins to them. Could you have ever imagined what a smart, perfect pairing they would make? Of course you could—you were their mother! And so, without the benefit of experience, or training, those two launched the *Tea Kettle Inn* on its road to success. Overnight restaurateurs! The tragedy is that you had so little time to bask in their success.

Only four years after Grandpa died, breast cancer took you, four months shy of your sixtieth birthday. Way too soon. Your heartbroken children wanted you to be with Grandpa, except the costly time commitment to accompany your remains to England was simply beyond their means. Above all, however, they would not hear of you sailing the seas unaccompanied. But a resourceful family finds a way, doesn't it? They sought assistance by spreading the word, and in no time a kind female traveller stepped forward. "I'm booked to sail to England this week," she said. "I'd be honoured to accept responsibility for Mrs. King on her final journey." That woman's generosity was never forgotten.

And so you travelled to England, where your Preston family received you, and arranged for your burial alongside Grandpa. The Kings rest in three locations: Arthur in Roclincourt Military Cemetery in France, where his grave is meticulously tended; you and Grandpa in England, adjacent to your Preston families; and the others in Canada—Calgary's historic Union Cemetery, where I regularly look in to make sure they are also tended. Rest well, Grandma.

Love you always,
Eleanor

Dear Uncle Walter,

It was a Sunday morning, and I came downstairs decked out in my new fall church attire, ready for Sunday School.

Getting to Know You

I was twelve years old. Mr. & Mrs. Stevenson, Mother and Dad's good friends, were our house guests at the time. They greeted me in the kitchen, looking strangely sombre. Mrs. Stevenson put her arm around me and ushered me into the dining room, where she sat me down and took my hands in hers. Then she told me the terrible news. "Your Uncle Walter had a severe heart attack in the night," she said. "He did not survive, dear. I am so sorry." I remember desperately wanting the comfort of my parents at that moment, but they were at your house, where they were needed most, of course. How was I supposed to deal with such news? I didn't know what to do with myself. So I went to Sunday School.

It was April 10, 1919, when you arrived back home in Canada, where you received your official discharge orders in Quebec City two weeks later—April 24. You carried with you the horrors of a barbaric war, visions you must have longed to un-see—a burden no 21-year-old should have to bear. And you were alone, with no one to share memories of a nightmare war, or concerns for what lay ahead. So you turned your focus to your immediate responsibility—preparing for your family's arrival to Calgary. You found a rental home and set to work scrabbling the accoutrements to make it livable. Did you get any sleep with all that excitement?

The family coming together in Calgary that first summer must have been a momentous occasion. What do you remember about that grand reunion? I wish I'd asked my dad about it, although I'm not sure if it's something he remembered. You, on the other hand, were not only an astute observer of life, but you had a steel trap memory. But since I have nothing concrete to go on, I'm at the mercy of my imagination. Here's what I see: the six of you sandwiched around a too-small table, diving into a pot of your mother's mouthwatering beef stew. Manners were temporarily forgotten, as hands reach across the table for one of Millie's hot biscuits, before she even had a chance to pass them. Your mother taught you better, but she turned a blind eye under the circumstances. You were all talking at once—so much news to share, but everyone too excited to listen. Your jubilation ended with nightfall, however. At the crack of dawn, I can hear Grandpa announcing, "Rise and shine! Time to get to work." Right? But he didn't have to pressure, did he? You were all keen to get on with the next chapter of your lives.

Now, you're not going to believe this, but I recently received a windfall—your next chapter all in your own handwriting! Your son Frank's widow, Jeanette, found your journal amongst Frank's effects, and thoughtfully lent it to me to browse. Your entries over the next years take my breath away. Moss certainly didn't grow under your feet. You began a teaching career, bravely taking on fall and spring terms at schools in an assortment of towns, some two-room schools, and some in which you proceeded directly to the position of acting principal. In-between postings, you furthered your education at the University of Alberta, where you marked grade school composition papers in the summers for extra income. For extracurricular activity, you ran (and won) one-mile or three-mile races, here and there. A mile in 4.54 is pretty good for an amateur. But in my books, the best thing you ever did was accept a teaching position for the 1924 fall term, at a little school in the town of Delia. That's where Mildred Mason, a warm and gentle fellow teacher, caught your eye, and swept you off your feet. You knew a good thing when you saw it, didn't you?

You married Mildred Laura Mason on September 2, 1926, at 12:30 p.m., in Delia, and had three children, who became beloved cousins of mine. I arrived a year after you had Frank, your third, and you and Aunt Mildred became my godparents. I remember Aunt Mildred with great fondness, as a calming influence in your household of boisterous sports fans. I have not forgotten her exquisite handicrafts—Christmas decorations galore, draping every square inch of the house, and her one-of-a-kind table cloths that graced your large dining room table—four of them—one for each season of the year. I loved crafting also, especially at Christmas, so I used to visit her regularly for new ideas. I don't need to remind you of the culinary spread that she produced at Christmas. Remember her sandwich loaves, far too beautiful to slice and eat? But we did anyway. And her melt-in-your-mouth Goosnargh cakes? Which brings to mind your wonderful house in Elbow Park, our favourite place to gather for food and games. And more food.

In recent years, the house was purchased by an interior decorator whose intention was to overhaul it for quick sale. One day, I spotted a photo of it in my morning paper—an open house advertisement. I called my daughter, Diane, to join me for a walk-through, although I feared that it might be unrecognizable now. Good news! It had been extensively renovated, including development of the second floor and the basement, but its basic layout and original charm had been meticulously preserved. I spoke to the attending owner/decorator, and told her of my history with the house. She was so excited to hear my tale of family Christmases in the home that she offered to turn it over to me for a week over Christmas. "You could invite your entire King family to gather and reminisce," she said. Can you believe such kindness? I gratefully declined, explaining that we couldn't possibly hold a King Christmas celebration in this home without Aunt Mildred's Goosnargh cakes. And you and I both know that no one on this earth has the wherewithal to replicate them.

Well, Uncle Walter, reading your journal, written after you married, was enlightening. You certainly had a varied employment record; there was nothing you didn't try or couldn't do. And you never stopped learning, whether it was further academic courses at U of A, cadet instruction courses in Calgary, or drama classes in Banff. And you were a writer! You wrote essays, which you entered into competitions, sometimes winning as much as $100.00. I'm flabbergasted to see that you were writing for pay the whole time I knew you—hundreds of articles for a plethora of publications. You specifically targeted youth, especially boys. Topics varied from athletes and athletics (especially runners and running), to sportsmanship, animals (caring for your dog, homing pigeons) and nature, (ancient trees, dinosaurs, cobwebs). You wrote war stories (heroes and heroines), and fiction, always with a morality message. And you openly shared your Christian beliefs writing for Christian publications—*Common Sense about Prayer, Changes in the Holy Land*. You wrote extensively about the laying of the first transatlantic cables joining Europe and America. You were particularly moved by the message of the first transatlantic telegraph on August 16, 1858: "*Glory to God in the highest; on earth, peace and goodwill toward men.*" I can't believe that I never knew you were a writer. How did this get past me? Did your siblings even know? Here we are, kindred spirits.

Beyond all this writing for publication, I also learned that you had built quite a reputation for ingenuity in Redcliff, as a teacher and school principal. Evidently, your school, which operated on a WWII budget, welcomed your resourceful ideas, such as wrapping combs with wax paper to make kazoos for music class, or sending the students outside in winter to collect rocks—consistent in size and weight—for use on a curling rink. Norma Sharpe, one of your students, has written about you inviting her French class to your home for dinner ... with a provision: the class could only speak French throughout the meal. She remembers when "the crunch of celery was the only sound at the table!"

During your Redcliff years you also served with the Auxiliary War Services, raising money for the war effort through entertainment enterprises. When the war ended in 1945, you moved your family to Calgary, where you lent your wisdom and experiences to the family businesses, the antique store and the restaurant. Later, you engaged a new business partner and entered the world of real estate. I was right when I said you could do anything, wasn't I?

Looking back, it surprises me that I have no memory of any contact with your family until you moved to Calgary. You were only 158 miles away in Redcliff! I guess the state of roads and cars back then, made 158 miles a lot farther than it is today. I've never forgotten the day that your family arrived. I couldn't contain my excitement—a new aunt and uncle and three more cousins! All that time, I had thought that my three *double* cousins down the street were all that I had. I was eight years old.

Only when I put it in writing today, has it occurred to me how little time you and I had together. You were taken from me—suddenly in the night—just five years after you entered my world. Five years! You were just fifty-two years old and I was five days shy of becoming a teenager. You must have been quite a guy for me to form such vivid memories of you in such a short time.

I look back on you as a loving, kind, and very funny guy, but additionally, someone extremely tense. Through mature eyes, I see a man wound tighter than a drum, and that saddens me. I now recognize the possibility that you may have been suffering the horrors of the war in steely silence throughout your life. I have learned that that was how it was for so many veterans. Men had to be men. We now know that the unseen injuries of war—shell shock or what today we call post traumatic stress disorder—is not a sign of weakness or lack of moral fibre, it is a physical manifestation of the inevitable, emotional stress of war. It is real. And we've learned that healing can only take place by acknowledging this, and opening up to loved ones. You survived the war, but I wonder if it didn't steal years from your life in the end. You were such a fit guy—wiry, a non-smoker, non-drinker, and a runner. Why were you taken so suddenly in the night at the age of fifty-two? Five years. That's all we had. Cheated. But they were good years weren't they!

Love you,
Eleanor

P. S. I just came across a comical note in Don's copious collection of family jottings, a story that took place just after your birth. A family friend named Walter Higgenson asked Grandpa if you were named after him. Grandpa, having especially avoided namesakes, said, "No, he's Walter after nobody!" The upshot was that as a boy you were frequently called "Walter-after-nobody." I wished I'd know that story before now. I would have loved calling you Uncle Walter-after-nobody! And we'd have laughed every time.

Dear Aunt Millie,

You had been failing over the past year, losing weight and a bit of your spark, but you never lost your warmth, your charm or your big beautiful smile. Now in your nineties, you were living in the familiar surroundings of the Bethany Care Centre, where Mother and Dad spent their last days. Everyone there loved you. Good heavens, what am I saying? Everyone everywhere loved you. I came often, and you'd laughingly entertain me with stories of your days working in the restaurant with Dad ... like the customer sitting at the counter, who put his false teeth in his glass of water while he sipped his coffee and read the menu. And the distressed customer seated near him, who pulled you aside and whispered, "Would you please tell that man to put his teeth in his mouth. The sight of them in that glass is spoiling my lunch!" Then one day when I arrived, the stories and the laughter were gone. You had declined dramatically, and I knew this day was going to be your last. So I curled up in a chair at your bedside, and stayed the night. You slipped away at daybreak, looking so serene. We were holding hands.

I am picturing you arriving in Calgary after the war, a beautiful twenty-year-old, chin up, shoulders back, ready to stride into a new life. You would have been an enormous help to your mother setting up housekeeping, and feeding your hungry brood of men, your dad and three brothers. You would have given your right arm to have had the fourth brother to feed. You loved Arthur so.

In the early days, you focussed on getting the family launched, assisting your mother with household tasks while helping your father establish and run his jewellery store. You always had a knack for seeing a need and stepping up to fill it. As family demands lessened, you found work clerking at *F. E. Osborne's* bookstore. Would you believe that thirty years after your worked there, I was purchasing my high school textbooks at the same store, and another thirty years after that, our youngest son attended F. E. Osborne school?

The next part of the family story intrigues me, how, in 1925, a nearby restaurant came up for sale, and the Kings up and bought it. Just like that! And then you and Dad were the ones who jumped in to run it. Just like that! It had always seemed a bit impulsive to me that you took on an exploit that complex with such haste and no experience. But since we both know what a success you made of it, I've had to look on it as courageous, rather than impulsive. The secret of your success was your recognizing, early on, the skills that you had—and didn't have—that would ultimately lead to your roles. I remember you telling me that your first act was to tell

Dad that you were hopeless with business affairs, so anything falling into that category was his. Conversely, cooking was not his forte, so that department was yours.

You became famous not only for your menus, recipes, and unbeatable cooking, but for your fastidious cleanliness, which became a major drawing card for your clientele. Remember when you lined up the waitresses before they went on duty, to inspect their hair (tucked into hairnets), nails (clean and clipped short with no chipped polish), and uniforms (fresh from the laundry)? When a friend told me that The *Tea Kettle Inn* was the only restaurant her mother would even consider eating at, because it was the only one in the city clean enough to meet her standards, I believed her. And you'll love this story: A few years ago, I connected with Kay, an engaging nonagenarian, who worked at the restaurant back in the '40s. She couldn't stop beaming when she reminisced about that time in her life, and her love and respect for you. "If Mrs. Snowdon spotted us touching our faces or our hair," she said, "she'd wave us off to wash our hands." Then laughingly, she added, "And she'd catch us every time." I'm amazed, Aunt Millie, that you understood the importance of hand-washing without any formal training in the matter.

You and Dad lost all the other members of your family so young. I was eternally grateful that you had each other well into your retirement years—a team to the end. I've never forgotten the day Dad died. It was as though the angel Gabriel summoned you that day. Dad was in long-term care, suffering late stage Parkinson's Disease. You were a regular visitor, usually Sunday afternoons. Then one Monday morning the care centre called me to say that he'd taken a sudden bad turn. I hopped in the car and raced over. Flying in the door, I encountered you busily removing your boots. "Aunt Millie!" I exclaimed, "What a surprise!" Visiting on a Monday morning was a complete departure for you—it was the day you always set aside for housework. On this particular Monday, a friend had called to say she was running errands in the vicinity of the centre, "if you would like to visit your brother." You decided yes, you'd take advantage of her offer for a lift. And there you were in your usual good cheer. How I hated dampening it with the bad news. We collected Mother, who resided in the same centre, and the three of us reached Dad's bedside in time for his final fifteen minutes. It was a perfect ending for him. The three women he loved most—his wife, his sister, and his daughter—at his side when he slipped away.

I only just learned through notes that Don left behind, that you met Uncle D that first summer after the war. Your friend Dorothy introduced you. Mother used to hint that, because he was American, he was not well received by the patriotic King family in the beginning. I can believe that, but I suspect they may have also held an attitude that no one was good enough for their only daughter and sister. Thank goodness he wasn't deterred—he knew a good thing when you saw it. And so did you. After a seven-year courtship, on August 16, 1926, you and DeWitt Emerson Snowden escaped to Vancouver and married. In my memory, the Kings wholeheartedly embraced him ... even though he was American. And he could sing! In fact, he launched one of the earliest barbershop quartets in the city.

It's shameful how little I ever got to know about Uncle D. He was simply my giant-sized uncle with the big, broad smile, infectious laugh, and size thirteen feet. I loved him to pieces. Since I selfishly possessed him as a full member of our family, I carelessly dismissed the fact that he had another family south of the border. Poor guy, really was stuck with us, wasn't he? Here I am now wishing I'd at least asked him about his US family. The only thing I learned was that he was twenty years younger than his closest sibling, which may have been a bridge too far.

Uncle 'D' second from left.

I know that you and Uncle D lived with an unfulfilled dream of having children of your own, he wishing for three beautiful daughters just like you, and you dreaming of three tall sons just like him. You had to settle for five nephews and four nieces, some tall, some short, and none particularly resembling either of you. You never treated us like poor substitutes, though—you adopted us as your own, and we thrived with that assurance. Did you realize that from the time I was twelve years old, Uncle D was my one and only uncle, which made him pretty special? But then he was special anyway.

I remember Uncle D standing in line all night, back in the '50s, for the chance to purchase a view lot on Britannia Drive, not with an eye to building an oversized, ostentatious home. The goal was a lovely little four-room bungalow to suit your quiet lifestyle. He was a commercial artist by trade, and extended his skills to painting mini murals directly onto the walls of your home, after painting the walls themselves that is. I remember him mixing paint colours—a dab of this and a dab of that—to get the perfect shade that he held in his mind's eye. Do you remember his answer when I once asked him what his favourite colour was? He said he loved any colour as long as it was green. I loved coming to visit you in your perfect little home. You were always smiling and waving from the kitchen window as I drove up the long driveway.

It may not surprise you to learn that after you were gone, the new owners of your home had it jacked up and carted away. They loved the beautiful setting, but there wasn't quite enough square footage to suit their needs. How I missed you waving me up the driveway from the window of your little bungalow. Now I could only drive by an unfamiliar split level with no one in the window. Then one day, when on a nostalgia drive-by, I discovered the split level was gone, if you can imagine. A third, larger home on a grander scale was under construction. I would learn that the new owner was none other than the *Calgary Flames* hockey superstar Jarome Iginla. I don't believe he's still the owner. I don't drive by any more.

I remember how you and Uncle D did everything together. You would accompany him to the corner hardware or paint store, and he never went out to the mountains to paint landscape alone—you were there to help him set up his easel. Remember the day you strolled up the Bow River, leaving him to paint undisturbed? You encountered a bear at pretty close range, and without a shred of knowledge about how to deal with the situation, you did it your way—you maintained eye contact and quietly talked to the bear while backing away slowly. "Nice bear. Oh, what a beautiful bear you are. I love the colour of your fur. Where are your children? Maybe you should look for them. Are they safe?" You claimed you had no reason to fear the bear; it knew you were a friend. Which of course, you were.

Uncle D, in turn, supported your keen interest in vitamins and minerals, regularly taxiing you to the health-food store. You were constantly reading up on the subject, and had become quite an expert. Friends often turned to you for advice on natural remedies for what ailed them, and you had a pretty impressive track record of successes. I'll confess that as kids we used to giggle at your lineup of vitamins, minerals, wheat germ bread, yoghurt (long before the public had even heard of it), and black strap molasses in your kitchen, though we never dismissed the fact that you perpetually glowed with good health. When Uncle D was stricken with a terminal spinal tumour, you kept him at home in your care to the end. As with the bear in the mountains, you instinctively knew all the right moves. I remember him repeating, "What did I do to deserve you?" I might ask the same question. We got lucky, didn't we, Uncle D?

The day you died, it was my turn to take care of you. What a privilege it was to spend the night at your side. You were peaceful and beautiful as always when you drifted off. Amen.

Love, love, love you!
El

P.S. I take my vitamins every day.

Dear Uncle Harry,

I was at my desk in Miss Allison's classroom—Grade 4—when a knock came at the door. Such an occurrence was out of the ordinary, so all us kids were wide-eyed and wondering *who?* When Miss Allison opened the door, I craned to see who, but the caller remained out of sight in the hallway. Then I heard his voice—the unmistakable voice of our beloved minister, Reverend Ashford. He had come to collect Ritchie, who, as you know, was also in my classroom. Even at that tender age, I sensed that something must be terribly wrong. And it was. Reverend Ashford was assigned the dreadful duty of telling Ritchie that his daddy was not coming home. You had undergone delicate brain surgery in Edmonton that morning, and you had not survived. The devastating news awaited me when I got home from school. It was the darkest day of my young life.

You were just nineteen years old when you landed in the big city—Calgary—after the war. My impression has been that you were the family dandy, decked out in suits from *Lingards*, a luxury unattainable by your brothers. In my mind's eye, I see you wearing smart British woollens for as long as I knew you, even on the tennis courts. I can't fathom how you played tennis in those long white flannel pants in a Calgary summer.

Then you stepped into a career that I think you were born for—teaching. All the neighbourhood kids adored you, and we nieces and nephews thought it was pretty special that you were ours. It was sort of like you were Dagwood and every kid was Elmo, the way you took an interest in us all, and knew how to communicate in our language. So off you went to North Calgary School where you taught for a few years, then to Colonel Walker School for many more. I picture you racing through math class so you could take the kids outside to play. Am I right? Then Grandma died and your life took a U-turn. The *House of Antiques* was in full throttle, and the family didn't break stride with their resolve to keep it running. You were appointed the designated driver.

That brings me to another one of those questions I never asked: Did you jump into this role willingly, or did you feel coerced? I only ask because I know that you would have been the most popular teacher in the city, and an antique business is quite a departure from teaching. Of course, you were good at antiques, too. (It seems to me, the Kings were good at whatever they decided to do.) By this time, too, Mother's baby sister was catching your eye. What took you so long?

You and Lillian married on September 19, 1930, and set up housekeeping in the 7th Avenue residence shared with the antique shop, now vacated by all other members of the family. Then you and your bride put your heads together to design your Scarboro Avenue dream home, which became a reality a year later. An early favourite memory of this home for me was its cozy kitchen nook for elbow-to-elbow eating with benches that lifted for storage. (Audrey has since confessed to me that she sometimes slipped the food she didn't want to eat into the storage bench beneath her. Uh oh, I've spilled the beans.) We loved the spacious, undeveloped basement, perfect for Don's theatrical creations. He organized a full stage with draw curtains, and rows of seating for our audience—the neighbourhood ladies. They clapped enthusiastically for every act. Outside, your garage held only gardening tools because you never owned a car. Your front hedge was the envy of the neighbourhood—you kept it meticulously clipped. The hill behind the house was full of prickly bushes, and, disappointingly, was too steep for hide and go seek or we could tumble all the way down to Twelfth Avenue.

I remember the excitement of coming all the way from our house in Connaught, for afternoon tea with Aunt Lil. Mother and I would get on the streetcar right in front of our house and get off twelve blocks later at the bottom of the hill below yours, where the streetcar circled back to retrace its route. In 1943, having lived the first sixteen years of their marriage in Connaught, my parents moved just down the street on Scarboro Avenue. Now we were two minutes away, which I loved, except I also loved riding on the streetcar, and now I didn't get to very often.

I know I was in the antique shop a number of times, but for some reason, memories of you in that setting have grown dim. I'm surmising it's because you were such a fun guy that my brain sort of dismisses you in a work setting. I do have a vivid memory of you walking home from work, which was your daily routine. More than once, I remember you appearing around the corner of the hill leading up to your home, and little Audrey, on spotting you, screaming down the hill to leap into your arms. We were all excited to see you rounding the corner. The fun uncle was here!

Lastly, I'll tell you about a very specific memory I have of you, one

I'm sure you wouldn't remember. You stopped by our house on your way home from church one Sunday—you were unusually late because you'd stayed to help with something or other at the church. You found me alone at the kitchen table, unenthusiastically dawdling over a soft boiled egg, the rest of the family having dispersed from lunch. You sat down beside me to chat, then picked up my eggshell, and peered inside. "Not quite clean," you said, pointing out specks of egg white still inside the shell. "See, over there." You handed it back to me, and I dug in my spoon, scraping vigorously to get every last morsel. You inspected it again, and without saying a word, reached into your shirt pocket for a pen. Then on the outside of the eggshell you wrote 100 percent, and handed it back to me with a broad, approving smile. Ever the teacher! I didn't get 100 percent from a teacher very often ... maybe another couple of times in spelling. But as I write to you about this story, I'm just now realizing that the reason I've likely remembered it all these years, is because it was the only moment that I ever had you all to myself. You, me, and a soft-boiled egg!

Then the clouds rolled in. Dad told me the story of untoward symptoms that you began experiencing—most notably the loss of strength in one arm—indicating that something wasn't quite right. But you had a business to run and a family to feed, and you were doing your level best to dismiss the problem. One day, Dr. Guy Morton, an Edmonton neurosurgeon, came into the restaurant for lunch while visiting the city. Dad was acquainted with Dr. Morton, having known his father, and quickly took matters into his own hands. Approaching Dr. Morton in the middle of his lunch, he said, "I'm concerned about my brother and would like you to see him right away." Dr. Morton responded kindly with a willingness to see you in his office in Edmonton as early as the coming week. But that was not what Dad had in mind. "That's kind of you," he said, "but I want you to see him right here, right now." He was already turning to collect you from the antique store. Poor Dr. Morton never had a chance.

Dad led the two of you down to his office in the basement, where Dr. Morton was obliged to at least perform a cursory examination. As it turned out, that's about all he needed to make a tentative, unwelcome diagnosis of a brain tumour. Further tests confirmed the diagnosis, and ultimately you underwent surgery in Edmonton. Unthinkably, we lost you. When my thoughts turn to that dark day, I grasp at the one bright light for me—that all three of your siblings accompanied you and Aunt Lil to Edmonton to lend support during that frightening time. The Kings really cared for their own, didn't they? The anguished return trip to Calgary without you must have been a grim reminder of the return to Canada without your beloved Arthur. Another brother was gone.

I was only in Grade 4 when you left us, too young to develop an adult relationship that I could hold onto for the rest of my life. And so I remember you in snatches—sort of mini movie clips. But they have stood the test of time: playing *Pom Pom Pull Away* at the coulee skating rink in winter; playing *War* in the coulee trenches in summer; fishing for Christmas presents over a hanging sheet in the corner of your kitchen with makeshift rods, reels, and hooks; and getting 100 percent on my eggshell. And, oh yes, I never pass the *Calgary Tennis Club* without seeing you decked out in those long, white flannel pants. You'd never believe what some players—even professionals—are wearing these days! Thankfully, good old Wimbledon still demands proper *whites*. Three cheers for the British.

I'll end on that note, but I'll write again. I know there'll be more questions.

Love you!
El

Dear Dad,

You arrived here after the war as a keen seventeen-year-old, with a significantly interrupted education, impatient to launch your working life without further delay. And so you plunged into your father's jewellery business, and learned the intricacies of watchmaking. I never knew this about you until I was maybe ten years old, watching you dismantle our old mantle clock (pun intended)—the one that was grand to look at, but didn't keep time. Now, I saw its million parts floating in linseed oil. Have I got that right? I think it was linseed oil. Anyway, as much as I had great faith in you, I was dead certain that you would never get that clock put back together. Fooled me, didn't you? One day, it appeared back on our mantle, ticking away in perfect time. I couldn't believe it. That's when Mother told me that you had learned watchmaking skills from your dad. She added, though, that you never liked it very much—handling all those tiny parts sort of got on your nerves. You were secretly pleased when your mother launched her own antique business, independent from the jewellery store, effectively putting an end to jewellery and watchmaking. By this time, you were twenty-two years old, and experiencing a new interest in your life.

You had become close friends with the Eustace brothers, who lived next door to the Anderson sisters. The day you spotted the elder of the two sisters, you asked your friend Stan for an introduction to "the girl I'm going to marry." Really, Dad? I know Mother was a catch, but I'm a bit skeptical about that story. How does a guy make such a wild prediction merely on first sight? I've often wondered what your friend Stan's response was. Did he eagerly introduce you, or was he hesitant? (Did Don ever tell you what he thought? He maintained through the years that your shy friend was always in love with Mother, and that you must have brazenly interfered with his objective. Some friend.) Well, it took a five-year courtship, but you fulfilled your prediction: on July 19, 1927, you married Ruby Anderson at the Pro Cathedral Church in Calgary, and thank goodness for that, or I wouldn't be here writing you this letter! And you did make up for stealing your friend Stan's girl by naming your firstborn after him. (And no one ever called my big brother "Stan-after-nobody," did they [inside joke!]?)

The next few years in your young life were pretty full. Imagine jumping into the restaurant business with limited to no experience in the food industry. That was almost as daring as predicting the girl you were going to marry even before meeting her. But you pulled off both, didn't you? I'll allow you all the credit for successfully getting Mother to the altar, but we both know that you couldn't have pulled off the restaurant business without the help of your sister. But, Dad, I'll keep that for another letter. In fact, there's so much I want to talk to you about, I promise I'll write at length again soon.

Till then ...
I'll keep loving you,
El

—Chapter Four—
Parents

Introduction

When setting out to write my parents, my immediate thoughts turned to the comforting years—the '40s and '50s—when we were all living together as a family. Dad's working world was managing a restaurant in downtown Calgary and Mother's working world was managing our household in our Scarboro neighbourhood. Revisiting those years has given me fresh insights into the simplicities—and complexities—of their lives. I've gotten to know them better. I could not write about their past worlds without giving them a peek at those worlds today. The landscape has changed, and the changes are moving faster than I am, but I'll do my best.

Father
Horace King

Born February 17, 1902—Preston, Lancashire, England
Died October 29, 1984—Calgary, Alberta, Canada

Dear Dad,

The morning you died, I lingered awhile in your room at the Bethany Care Centre, gathering my thoughts of our life together. You had suffered from Parkinson's Disease for over twenty-five years, and been wheelchair-bound for the past seven. You had stayed pretty independent until you fractured your hip from a fall, which led to one failed surgery after another. You had been through the wringer, hadn't you? Blessedly, you were spared any sign of dementia, a condition that frequently accompanies Parkinson's, so we enjoyed meaningful times together to the end.

When you were first diagnosed back in the late fifties, the disease seemed less prevalent than it is now, and we (meaning the family) found ourselves travelling down a lonely, unfamiliar road. We had no idea where it would lead us. Still, it wasn't fear of the unknown that troubled me the most, it was the rapid change in your personality that I witnessed. You were the guy who never gave in to anything, the guy who didn't see problems, only solutions. I agonized watching you. It seemed to me that you were surrendering to the potential of your disease before challenging it. Even today, knowing that anxiety commonly comes hand in hand with Parkinson's Disease, I can't help wondering whether you gave up the business that you loved too soon. Whether keeping a foot in the door might have given you continued purpose. But I also know that it's not fair of me to judge.

Now, having said all that, as I held your hand on that chilly October morning, all the questions and uncertainties seemed to vanish, and I was buoyed by memories of the vibrant dad that I first knew. The dad who jumped out of bed at the crack of dawn, when the rest of us were pulling the covers over our heads. The dad who, unthinkably, splashed in a cold bath to get his day underway, then bounced down the stairs to the breakfast table, full of vim and vigour. The funny, energetic, enthusiastic dad, who loved life. How comforting it was to know that, in spite of the rigours of Parkinson's Disease, yours was a life that got lived.

This might be a good time to mention that, after you died, I took up freelance writing. I must have acquired the writing bent from you. My first book, entitled *The House With The Light On*—the *house* referring to our Scarboro address—was a memoir of growing up in Calgary in the '40s and '50s. I devoted the last chapter to the *Tea Kettle Inn*, and you wouldn't believe the number of people who bought the book for that chapter alone. The restaurant lives on. If only you'd been here for the book's launch, you'd have found yourself surrounded by your old waitresses, including Kay Wilson, who gathered the group for the occasion. And of course you'd remember Louise, the laughing cook, and quiet Ann, who worked in the bakery. Her two sisters also worked at the restaurant, and you gave all three of them away at their weddings.

A few weeks after the launch, Kay called, inviting me to lunch. I was overjoyed. When I arrived at her cozy—and spotless—home, she greeted me bursting with stories she couldn't wait to tell. So I settled in, and she began with the beginning. She came to the big city when she was scarcely twenty years old, to attend the Prophetic Bible Institute, located on Calgary's 8th Avenue. Leaving home for the first time was terrifying for a shy farm girl from Hanna, but she bravely made her way into her new world, making friends and getting acquainted with the city. Keen to establish her independence, she set out to find a job that would accommodate her school schedule. Night work in a bakery was the perfect answer. Except ... not so perfect.

Kay still cringed at the memory of that job, especially the spectacle of her workmate—a male baker—who she described as turning up for his shift looking like he didn't own a shower or a washing machine. She's never been able to erase the memory of his sweaty chest clad in a stained undershirt, and "oh those hairy underarms," she gasped. She did her best to ignore his unsavoury demeanour, until the day he casually demonstrated his efficient method for icing the donuts: "He plunged his big hairy arm into a vat of prepared icing," she said, squirming, "and swept it across a large tray of donuts." She resigned that day. The next day, she filled out an application to work at the *T Kettle Kounter*, your place on 6th Street. She was hired on the spot.

"When I walked in there for my first day of work," she said, "my heart just sang at the sight of everything sparkling. I knew this was the place for me." Countless people have told me that a drawing card for eating there was its cleanliness, but Kay is the first person to proclaim cleanliness as the reason she chose to work there.

Kay was full of stories. She couldn't contain the giggles when telling me about free-spirited Juline, a fellow waitress who seemed to be plowing through life without a worry in the world. You'll remember that the restaurant had swinging doors between the dining room and the kitchen, and staff had been trained to always take the doors on the right whether coming or going. Evidently, poor Juline couldn't seem to grasp this concept. Every morning, like clockwork, a particular businessman arrived on the dot of eight o'clock, always seating himself at the same table near the swinging doors, to be in Kay's station, and always ordering the same breakfast: scrambled eggs on toast. Kay had grown fond of this pleasant patron, and went out of her way to start his day with her best service. One morning, when Kay was arriving from the kitchen carrying her favourite customer's breakfast, Juline hit the same door full force from the other side. Kay's customer was wearing scrambled eggs. Mortified, she attempted to brush the yellow curds from his meticulously pressed navy suit, while Juline giggled off into the kitchen, through the wrong door—without even egg on her face.

Another time, Juline phoned Kay to say she was suffering from a bad case of impetigo, a bacterial skin infection, and to ask if Kay would please tell Mr. King that she would not be able to come to work that day. Kay is still laughing at your response: "I don't know what impetigo is," you said, "but it sounds like something Juline would get." That sounds like something you'd say, Dad!

Kay especially loved the camaraderie amongst fellow staff members, doing typical girl things together between shifts, like shopping and discussing diets. "You talked diets?" I said. "In a restaurant?"

"Oh, yes," she giggled. "And Louise, the jolly cook, was the most famous dieter." "Let's start a diet tomorrow," Louise would say to anyone listening. "We'll start the day with Alka Seltzer, then one muffin for breakfast and an apple for lunch." I suggested to Kay that Louise's diet didn't work. I remember her as being lovingly round, a figure that perfectly suited her occupation and spirited disposition.

Another lasting memory for Kay was her wedding reception for thirty-five people, which she held at the *Tea Kettle Inn*. "My restaurant family did a wonderful job for me," she said, adding with a big grin, "A dollar a plate!" Most touching for me, Dad, was Kay's memory of your kindness to all the staff. "Many of the girls were from farms like myself," she said, "and this was a safe haven for us. Your dad was so patient, never abrupt, and we always felt cared for." Your staff developed a sisterhood, Dad. They became a family. Would you believe that, in 1990, more than thirty years after the restaurant closed, twenty-four "sisters" gathered to reminisce? What a beautiful legacy you left.

Since publishing the book, further restaurant staff have popped into my life, always excited to tell me their story: "Working for your dad was my first job. I was so scared, but he put me at ease." "My mother was a cook at your dad's restaurant for many years." "You have a picture in your book of your dad with a group of waitresses in front of the *Tea Kettle Inn*. My mother's in the back row." And I'll never forget the day that I had a book table at Fort Calgary's Remembrance

Day event when a lovely couple stopped to tell me that each of their mothers had worked at the restaurant, one as a baker and the other a dishwasher. They were proud of their mothers' honourable work, and knew how much you valued their contributions to the business.

Countless past patrons of the restaurant phoned or wrote to offer stories of their particular memories. Farm folk had a common thread: "We came in from the country every Saturday, purchased our week's supplies, and went to the *Tea Kettle Inn* for tea before going home. Our routine never changed." City folks' stories varied a bit more: "I remember my mother dressing up in her best dress, hat, and gloves, and catching the Killarney bus to go downtown for tea at the *Tea Kettle Inn*." "The *Tea Kettle Inn* was where I had my first date with my husband-to-be. You didn't mention the wonderful fried oysters, which were our favourite thing." (Sorry, Dad, but I don't remember the fried oysters.) "I loved the *Tea Kettle Inn*. My favourite item on the menu was clams." Clams? I don't remember them either. But I do remember John, my old neighbourhood pal. Do you? I recently reconnected with him at a gathering of past Scarboro residents, where he announced to all in earshot that I was his first girlfriend. "I'd take Eleanor to a movie," he exclaimed, "then after, she'd take me to her dad's restaurant for a free soda." I had the good sense not to ask John which was the greater attraction—me or the free soda.

Finally, you won't believe how many people asked about the neon sign—the hanging tea kettle over the front door: "I loved the

restaurant's neon sign. Whatever happened to it?" I've never been able to answer that question, Dad, can you? I assumed that it was destroyed when the restaurant closed in '58, but I still hold a glimmer of hope that it was secretly stashed in someone's garage somewhere, maybe lying beneath a mountain of other prized collectibles, awaiting the day of reckoning when the owners' offspring were dispensing with their parents' treasures. "A neon tea kettle? And we thought we'd seen everything!"

So, you sold the building to *National Bakery*, which operated from the premises for many years. You'll also remember that the bakery added a second floor, and the building became known as the *Heagle Building*. Ultimately, your old site lived out its final days as a *Dollar Store*. But it was Calgary's downtown development in the 2010s that delivered the ultimate kiss of death.

One morning in 2013, I opened my newspaper to discover a rendering of a proposed $1.3 billion, fifty-six-storey office tower, targeted to rise on the corner down the street from us. Unthinkable! That property had been occupied by the *Calgary Herald* my whole life. The *Herald* people were like family. When I cashiered for you one summer, I remember the *Herald* staff pouring into the restaurant en masse for their coffee breaks and lunches. Always under the gun to meet deadlines, they had no time to stand in line waiting for the cashier to ring up their respective charges, so they plopped their chits on the counter top, tossed loose change on top, and flew out the door, back to work. I spent the next twenty minutes ringing up the charges, praying the cash was going to balance with the chits. The thing is, it rarely did. The good *Herald* people always left more than enough to cover. And they never forgot their waitress; they slipped a dime for her under their coffee cup.

The article described this new development as *Brookfield Place*, a complex of buildings and plazas that would consume the entire block between 1st and 2nd streets and 6th and 7th Avenues. That meant we were really doomed to disappear now. So I dashed downtown to see the goings on with my own eyes. My heart sank when I found the *Heagle Building* gutted, waiting in ghostly silence for someone to finish the job. With a heavy heart I caught the first C-train back home.

A few days later, I steeled myself for a return trip to the scene. This time, the *Heagle Building* was gone—not a trace left of us, Dad. Gone, too, were all the neighbouring buildings to the east, including the beautiful *J. J. Fitzpatrick Block*. Walking on the south side of the street, I slowly moved past the long stretch of emptiness, my mind's eye pleading for the old familiar streetscape. As I neared the corner, the sight confronting me brought on a visceral response—our beloved *Herald* building was under vicious assault at the hands of a monstrous set of mechanical jaws. They were ripping it to shreds. I leaned back against the *Bay*, blinking back the tears. People nonchalantly walked past me—back and forth, back and forth—without raising an eyebrow or turning a head. An entire block of Calgary's history was unceremoniously erased from the map, yet not one soul was giving it a thought. No one even slowed their pace to ponder our past. I felt a bit

like the last surviving soldier after a war—the only one left standing to remember how it was. Well, if it's any comfort, Dad, I have preserved the *Tea Kettle Inn* for posterity on paper.

Gone!

Replaced by …

Before I leave the topic of the restaurant, I want to assure you that I haven't forgotten your ventures beyond the original *Tea Kettle Inn*. In the '40s, you had four other operations on the go: a *T Kettle Kounter* on 8th Avenue, west of the *Palace Theatre*, which operated for six years, targeting the lunch trade, and a second *T Kettle Kounter* on 6th Street over in the Beltline, which was turned over to the more specialized *Harris Sky Room* after two years. For a brief time, your friend Ken managed *Malzard's*—named for Ken's middle name—across from the old post office on 8th, where Aunt Millie served up her *chicken in the straw*, a specialty Colonel Sanders could never top ... and hasn't. *Malzard's* also had a soft ice cream machine that served up an indulgence that was relatively new at the time. Then around 1950, you conceived, planned, designed, and constructed *The Carolina* on Centre Street, a joint venture with the Mottishaws—Reuben and his son Roy. The Mottishaws were outstanding partners, and Aunt Millie brought her chicken in the straw with her. Calgarians loved *The Carolina*, didn't they? It goes without saying that your interests extended beyond your own business to others in the downtown. I wish I'd been around back in the '30s when you launched *The Tea Kettle Inn Kritics Klub*, a weekly gathering of local downtown businessmen, who met in the basement of the restaurant to discuss issues of the day. Your *Klub* would not believe the changes in the downtown since then. There's far too many to fit into one letter, but I know you'd want to hear about the ones that touched you and me the most.

Let's begin with the four downtown theatres that drew in our family every Saturday night. For starters, the single-screen theatres that we loved so, no longer exist. They've been replaced by multiplex facilities that house eight to ten small theatres, all running different films simultaneously. I assume it makes technical and financial sense, but they sure don't have the ambiance of the old, ornate theatres.

The *Capitol* on 8th, our favourite, was demolished back in the '70s to make way for a shopping mall. But then you were here to mourn that sad event with me. *The Palace* across the street from the *Capitol* hung in until the late '90s, when it became *Flames Central* for nine years, a sports bar and grill where fans of our National Hockey League team, the *Calgary Flames*, gathered under big-screen TVs with a beer to cheer on the home team. The original contractors, building the theatre in 1912, would have been amused by the modern moniker *Flames Central*—they had famously boasted that their construction was *absolutely fireproof*. A few years ago, it reverted back to its original name, the *Palace Theatre*. But Dad, not for movies—it's a live music venue offering loud—very loud—music with stage lasers and strobe lighting that I'd swear could trigger a seizure. Not your style or mine.

And of course you'd never forget the dear old *Grand* around the corner, or the days back when it primarily housed live theatre, and you'd willingly stay up all hours to meet and greet the cast members that habitually came to the *Tea Kettle* for their post-performance nosh. You even prepared a special late-night menu just for them. Well, those of us who'd grown attached to the old *Grand* had some years of anxiety when it seemed destined for destruction. Was I pleased when Calgary's *Theatre Junction Society* came to the rescue in 2005. Its members redesigned it into multi-purpose spaces for cultural and theatrical events, and to accommodate corporate or private functions as well. They renamed it the *Theatre Junction Grand*. I took Don, our own theatre aficionado, to see it one day, and he was horrified at its garish new look. He couldn't escape fast enough. He really doesn't like historic, ornate craftsmanship messed with, does he? Twelve years later, *Theatre Junction* departed, and new management brought back its original name. And so, the *Grand* continues as an active member of the Calgary arts scene.

A latecomer to the downtown scene was the *Uptown Theatre*—last to come and last to go. Do you remember when the family went to the *Uptown* together, either opening night or soon after, in March 1951? I probably didn't tell you, but as a fourteen-year-old, I wasn't all that excited about the choice of location—way out west past 5th Street, wasn't familiar territory for me. My comfort zone was between 1st and 3rd. But you were game for anything, anywhere, of course, and a new theatre was a pretty special occasion.

You were dazzled with the *Uptown*, especially its size, and its oversized balcony. Also, it was housed in Calgary's first skyscraper, the Barron Building. I don't remember the first movie we saw there, but I'd bet my bottom dollar that you could. You could probably replay it frame by frame in your mind's eye, too. You could do that with every movie you saw. The *Uptown* delivered some great movies to Calgarians for a lot of years, then it died a slow death in its declining skyscraper. It was finally shuttered in 2012. Ten years later, though, the *Barron Building* has become the talk of the town again. A local *Strategic Group* is converting it to residential units, with retail space on the main floor, and parking underground. And the good news is, they're executing the project while preserving the integrity of the building and its beautiful heritage facade. Are you smiling?

Your downtown focus was understandably on 7th Avenue, but for me the heart of downtown was the corner of 8th Avenue and 1st Street West, where I got off—and on—the Sunalta bus. Lois and I would take the bus downtown on a Saturday, get off on that corner, and step into the *Bay* colonnade. Within minutes we'd run into someone we knew.

Today, I could stroll that colonnade all day and never see a familiar face. Where did everybody go? I've become one of those Calgarians who waxes lyrical about Calgary's *best days* being in the '50s, but the fact is, it's true. That was hands down the best time and place to be a kid.

A typical shopping excursion for me started on 8th and 1st with the *Bay*, where I bought all my sweaters with my babysitting money. But I haven't forgotten the one time that you and I did the *Bay* together. You'd been shopping previously and selected a lovely set of hard-sided luggage (white) for my nursing school graduation gift, but you wanted my approval before making the purchase. The salesman helping us was the same man that had helped you initially, but he didn't have the good sense to concede that he'd effectively sealed the deal already. So he set about launching a whole new pitch, bragging about the durability of this amazing new *Samsonite* luggage. With dramatic flair, he laid the largest suitcase on its side, and invited you to stand on it. So you did. The suitcase withstood your weight, and the salesman beamed from ear to ear. I've never forgotten the look on his face, though, when you asked, "Now can I jump on it?" We left the *Bay*, me happily carrying a small white suitcase and you carrying its matching larger one. Neither had been jumped on.

Just west of the *Bay* was *Robert's Shoe Store*, positively the last word in shoes. And, oh, their enticing window displays. I rarely worked up the courage to step inside, and when I finally did, a clerk eyeing me critically from head to toe did nothing to relieve my insecurity. I still managed to splurge in *Robert's* on two occasions, once for a trendy, comfortable pair of *Corey* shoes, blue suede flats with tassels—all the rage in high school—and the second time for my first pair of high heels—black suede, very high, and cripplingly uncomfortable.

They made their debut the next morning when I hobbled to church in them, where I scarcely heard the sermon over the noise of my screaming feet. Returning home, the pain became unbearable, so I took them off and walked the last block carrying them, shredding my Sunday-best nylon stockings on the rough sidewalk. I wore those shoes on only one other occasion—with the same drastic result. At least I got my money's worth with the comfy *Coreys*. I wore them regularly for years.

West of the *Capitol Theatre* stood the two five and dime stores, *Woolworths* and *Kresge's* in close proximity to one another. It wasn't particularly cool for us snobby teenagers to be seen in the five and dimes, so I mostly relegated them to Mother, who wasn't under peer pressure to look cool. I remember her heading down to *Woolworths* with her list of *notions*, her word for small articles such as hair brushes, bobby pins, sewing needles, thread, buttons, ribbon, and such. Whatever happened to *notions,* anyway? I've not heard that word in years. I also remember her buying our toothbrushes there, which she plucked unpackaged from an open bin. Remember how she soaked them in boiling water in her Pyrex measuring cup on the kitchen counter? They'd be immersed there all afternoon, until she deemed them fit for human consumption. She sure looked after us, didn't she, Dad?

Liggett's Drugstore stood on the corner of the next block, the place I entered with only one mission—to examine, through a magnifying glass, the sheet of thumbnail photos taken by the street photographer. I assume he must have developed them in the back of the store. Lois and I would scream with delight when we found ourselves in miniature, and deemed it worthy of ordering a 4x6 print. Today, Dad, people are taking their own photos with their cell phones—they call them *selfies*. It's technological wizardry, I suppose, but they miss out on the excitement of waiting for a week, then finding themselves in the drugstore. And *selfies* just get buried on cell phones, lost to the world after the first viewing. The carefully selected street photos of the '50s found a place of honour within albums and memoirs for all time.

Hollingsworth's Ladies Wear stood across the street from *Liggett's*. Don't tell Mother, but I sort of looked down my nose at *Hollingsworth's*, because its apparel looked mostly old-ladyish to me—suitable for Mother's age group at best. But the truth is, when I fished through their racks carefully, I frequently found a skirt or a blouse there that suited my sixteen-year-old taste. The original *Birks Jewellery Store* was also in this block, but I only entered its revolving door for special occasions. I bought my school rings there, and Don and I purchased Mother's Christmas gift there one year, a beautiful Czechoslovakian crystal necklace with matching bracelet and earrings. She loved it. After she died, I discovered a bundle of small boxes carefully stowed in one of her dresser drawers. Each box contained a piece of jewellery, designated for each female member of the family, and each piece was accompanied by a handwritten note describing its history. She chose Cousin Ethel to receive her Czechoslovakian Christmas set. Ethel was deeply touched by the gesture, but graciously insisted that it belonged with me. So it has come back home.

My other memory of Mother and *Birks* was accompanying her there to shop for a wedding gift, pretty much her exclusive reason for shopping there. The big drawing card for me was not helping her choose the gift, however, but watching, in awe, the store's unique method of handling the transaction, always with cash—credit cards had not yet arrived on the scene. The clerk would tuck Mother's cash into a small tube, which she'd then place inside a larger, clear vacuum tube that ran from her workstation to the office. With the press of a button the money tube was sucked from sight. The clerk would then set about the task of gift wrapping, and by the time she was done, the tube containing the change and the receipt had magically returned. I loved watching that process.

Heintzman and Co. Music Store, across the street from *Birks*, was a favourite place where Lois and I would hang out for hours, checking out all the new vinyls. We'd drive the clerks crazy asking them to play selections for us, which we'd listen to in small cubicles at the back of the store. I hate to think how many times we left the store without making a single purchase. Why would we when we'd already done the week's hit parade in the back booth?

In the next block you'll remember *Eaton's* department store, the *Bay's* main competition. Except for me as a teenager it ran a distant second. Years later when I was a newlywed, however, it rose to number one. I purchased a twenty-three-dollar used wringer washer in *Eaton's* basement, which came with a year's warranty and free delivery. Its labouring gyrator screeched to a halt one month before the warranty ran out. A serviceman came promptly and restored it to life. He didn't charge a dime. *Eaton's* closed in 1988.

Only a handful of stops drew me east from my 1st Street corner, the first being the beautiful *Bank of Montreal* on the corner, across from my bus stop. I used to accompany Mother there to deposit her family allowance cheques. She taught me how to fill out a deposit slip, and depositing was the only thing I saw her do there. I never saw her withdraw money. So I grew up with the mindset that banks were for depositing your money only. When I began earning my own through babysitting and summer jobs, I was proud as punch to open my first account at Mother's *Bank of Montreal*. And I was the best little saver in the world, because I would withhold a portion of my earnings for my spending money, then put the rest into my account where it would stay in perpetuity. Unfortunately, the bank did not stay in perpetuity—it closed its big beautiful brass doors in the mid-nineties, making way for a fabulous music store—*A & B Sound*—to waltz in. Ten years later, A & B's crop of CDs was replaced with free weights and treadmills by *Goodlife Fitness*! It's the most elegant fitness centre I've ever seen, with its thirty-five-foot ceiling embossed with golf leaf. And outside, it still has its commanding facade with the frieze bearing *Bank of Montreal* above the four fluted columns. Mother doesn't need to know about the unseemly red *Goodlife Fitness* banner running conspicuously up the front face. Let's agree not to tell her.

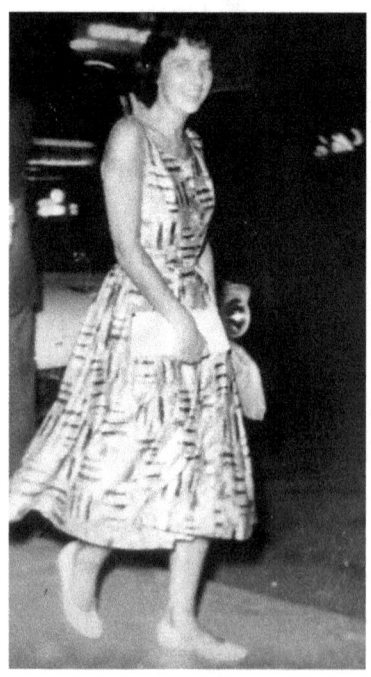

Just past the bank was the *Betty Shoppe,* where I occasionally found an item to buy with money that didn't get deposited in the bank next door. I especially remember a sleeveless summer dress that I bought there—a beautiful rich blue with red piping that buttoned down the front. I absolutely loved that dress. The street photographer captured me in it one day, although the black-and-white photo didn't catch the colour that I loved best about the dress. I never did know who *Betty* was.

Spence's Shoes, just past the *Betty Shoppe,* was Mother's go-to place for getting my school shoes. She insisted on practical shoes for developing feet, and *Spence's*, with its X-ray machine, was the one place where we could be properly fitted. The clerk would measure my feet, fit me with the appropriate size, and then place my feet in the machine, where I could look through my own portal and see the outline of my toes in relation to the soles of the shoes. The fascinating X-ray machine was the only drawing card to *Spence's* for me, because I knew I was in for another dreaded pair of oxfords there—*Sisman Scampers* is the name that comes to mind. Those ugly shoes met their death in high school, though. I stamped my feet and refused to wear them.

The English Shop down on the corner of 8th and Centre Street was Calgary's answer to *Harrods*, boasting two floors of fine British woolens presented in exquisite oak display cases. It was a rare occasion when I ventured in—just to look—because only those with champagne tastes and budgets to match actually shopped there. With the exception of Don, whose budget scarcely qualified, but since he had champagne tastes, he shopped there anyway.

And finally, on the south side of the street across from the *English Shop* was the *Silkolina Fabric Shop*, where Mother and I waded through bolts and bolts of fabric for our sewing projects. Mother was a skilled seamstress, as you know, but that doesn't mean she particularly liked sewing. In fact, I suspected otherwise because it always took her forever to complete a project. Do you remember her sewing on the final hook of my Grade 12 prom dress while I was in it, dancing with anxiety because my date was ringing the doorbell? No offence, Dad, but I was pretty anxious about leaving him in your clutches any longer than necessary!

Well, there you have it—all my favourite places gone. Except the good old *Bay*, with its colonnade of strangers.

You probably know that Mother frowned on me ever going east of Centre Street, because she deemed it unsafe. So for all my growing up years, my world ended at Centre. If she could see me now! A whole new, beautiful world has opened up in her forbidden territory.

We could start with the *Glenbow Museum*—bordering on 1st Street East—formed in the '60s with Eric Harvie's donation of his vast collection to the people of Alberta. Its archives are now one of the largest in Canada. It's currently undergoing a massive, multi-million-dollar, three-year renovation. Mother would definitely give it a thumbs up, in spite of its address. Across the street east from the Glenbow is our multi-theatre complex, *Arts Commons*, taking up the whole city block from 1st to 2nd Streets East, between 8th and 9th Avenues. Remember the old post office, with its beautiful marble columns and floors? Well, it's been incorporated into the *Commons*, and the magnificent *Jack Singer Concert Hall* resides in its space. The *Jack Singer* has been described as one of the most beautiful and acoustically acclaimed venues in North America. There are five other live theatres within the *Commons*, and, Dad, I haven't forgotten your love of live theatre. This place would knock your socks off!

Adjacent to the *Commons* running along its north side, lies *Olympic Plaza*, installed for Calgary's 1988 Winter Olympics. That's right—the Olympics—would you believe? And not only that, Cousin Frank spearheaded the whole affair. But then, that might not surprise you—you've always recognized the endless capabilities of our Frank. Mother was never much of a sports fan, so she'd be surprised—and pleased—with the five bronze statues that have been awarded a prominent place on the southwest corner of the Plaza. The statues depict the brave women who challenged British Canadian law to include women as *persons*—Emily Murphy,

Henrietta Edwards, Irene Parlby, Louise McKinney, and Nellie McClung. We call them the *Famous Five*. I know that Mother would be familiar with them all—she followed their battles and achievements with interest and gratitude. You'll remember when she wrote Nellie McClung to tell her so—and received a handwritten reply. Mother cherished her right to vote, finally won on a historic day in 1929, and she never failed to exercise that right from that day forward.

Right next to the *Famous Five* is *Teatro Restaurant*, which inhabits the old Dominion Bank Building. It's famous for its ambience as well as its food, the owners displaying their own taste in art, while retaining the building's original Beaux-Arts architecture. But there's been a bit of a hike in prices over time. When I last checked, a dinner rib-eye was running sixty-five dollars. I still have a copy of your 1949 *Tea Kettle Inn* special menu for Stampede week. Your top item was *Choice Alberta T-Bone Steak* at $1.65.

Then if you make your way farther east, you'll be in our *East Village*. On 3rd Street East is our spectacular, world-class *Central Library*, an oval-shaped building, four floors in height with eye-catching glass panels dotting its exterior. It's elevated above street level to allow the CTrain to run beneath it. Inside, an enormous atrium runs the full height throughout the centre, topped by a skylight. I can't begin to do it justice in this letter, but I think you can tell that I'm pretty pumped with this fantastic addition to the city.

Then one block farther east to 4th, you'll find the historic *King Edward Hotel*, now meticulously restored—brick by brick—sharing space with *Studio Bell*, new home of the *National Music Centre*, a museum and performance facility dedicated to showcasing Canada's musical past, present, and future. In addition to the museum, the Centre holds a 300-seat performance theatre, a radio station, and recording facilities to support new talent. Sometimes I can't believe what's cropped up in this city since my youth.

The rest of the *East Village*, running all the way to 6th Street East and from 9th Avenue to the river, offers every business imaginable to serve your every need. Which includes food, of course. The pizza parlours, coffeehouses, burger bars, and grilles are a departure from the *Tea Kettle Inn*, Dad, but you'd have a heyday checking them out. Mother, by the way, would be gobsmacked by this charming corner of the city. Please tell her that it's safe for me to walk past Centre Street now.

Finally, the Beltline, our old neighbourhood—I've actually heard it referred to as downtown, but I'll never bring myself to calling it that. We always defined downtown as north of the railroad tracks and their underlying subways, didn't we? In any event, I know how much you loved walking, and a walk in the Beltline today would take on a whole new dimension for you. It's become famous for its fabulous street

art, known as *BUMP— Beltline Urban Murals Project*—colourful works on building exteriors, everywhere you look. One standout mural, and by far the tallest, is a rendering of an enormous cougar, painted by South African artist Liberty Du, who goes by the name Faith 47. You'll never believe where it's located! It runs all the way up the side of the condo building that stands smack on the corner of 7th

Street where our first home once stood. We've been supplanted by a cougar!

But the story you'll never believe is the one surrounding the lovely old *President Apartments* across the street from us. New owners wanted to build a new condo complex on the popular corner, but were pressured to retain the *President's* heritage designation. So architects came up with an ingenious solution—they'd raise the original building from its foundation and move it onto 7th Street while they constructed the new complex. On completion, they'd nestle the old, preserved building back into place adjacent to the new. I thought the idea was some kind of a joke, except they seemed pretty serious. Not surprisingly, the idea was eventually scrapped, and our beloved *President Apartments* stand in place unscathed. But if anyone wants an example of what that project may have looked like, they only need to walk one block west to where my old sandstone high school has joined hands with the shiny new eight-floor *Board of Education* office building.

Central High closed as a high school just ten years after I graduated, due to declining enrolment. Imagine! In 1955, 500 of us were swarming the place, and, ten years later, there weren't enough kids to keep the doors open. So the school moved in new directions, housing temporary elementary classes in the beginning, then meeting the special needs of students with developmental disabilities. Some years later, it was re-commissioned as an *Adult Education Centre*, and, later still, it was leased to *Rundle College*, a private school. In its final calling, as *The Carl Safran Centre*, its hallowed halls house some *Board of Education's* administration offices.

I went for a nostalgia walkabout there recently, and, I have to say, the view from 12th Avenue was kind of depressing—because there wasn't one. The big new *Board of Education* building, butting up against our old majestic sandstone, was blocking it from sight. So much for nostalgia! Not only that, our beloved gymnasium—the venue for our basketball games and Friday night dances—was gone! Not just hiding—gone. I have to confess, I didn't know until after the gymnasium was demolished, that it had been noted for its *Egyptian revival* style—whatever that is. I doubt that I'd have paid much attention to that tidbit of information when I was a student anyway. But the piece of information that now had my attention was the fact that the gymnasium was built in 1940. Dad, it was younger than me! And discarded like so much trash! So I went looking for good news on the other side of the school. And I found some.

The 13th Avenue (South) side was most familiar to me, being the side I came and went from every day for three years. I found it filled with lush greenery dispersed with unfamiliar tables and benches that invited me to sit and stay awhile, contrary to the dictates of our principal. He did not want us to sit and stay awhile—he wanted us to go home. And on the west side, our rugged schoolyard, prey to the pounding feet of football practices and other athletic pursuits, was now covered in pristine grass. The high chain-link fences that had surrounded the yard had been removed to make it readily accessible for residents of the community to come and go. I couldn't help wondering what Mr. Weir, our old principal, would think of the bikini-clad sun worshipper, basking on her towel on the fifty-five-yard-line of our football field.

Well, Dad, I could talk about the changes in this city endlessly, but since I have to stop somewhere, I suppose *cougar corner* is as good a place as any. As I wind this up, though, I've been turning my thoughts to your King family, and the one common attribute that I think defined you all best— your zest for life. I don't picture any of you ever standing still—you were a gang on the move. Sadly, with the exception of you and Aunt Millie, the Kings did not enjoy long lives. The men—your father and all three brothers—failed to reach the age of fifty-five, and your mother died just shy of sixty. Yet I'm sure you'd agree that none of them wasted their limited days drifting along—they went through life full bore. As did you and Aunt Millie, left to carry the King banner together.

I'm especially thinking about the diverse involvements that filled the lives of the King siblings outside their workdays: Uncle Walter was a competitive distance runner, although he sat still long enough to write copious articles and poetry for publication; Aunt Millie was a lifelong learner and promoter of wellness, health food products, and vitamins; and Uncle Harry—proficient at tennis—was a sports enthusiast who spearheaded the development of recreation facilities in the neighbourhood. And that brings me to you, and your complete dedication to Moral Re-Armament (MRA), the Christian-based ideology that came into your life in the thirties, and swept you off your feet. It became the bedrock of your life, and you became a leading spokesman for its cause.

Originating in England, MRA endorsed four main principles—purity, honesty, unselfishness, and love—admirable standards for us all to adhere in our daily lives. By adding the word *absolute* to each of these standards, MRA left no room for grey areas or excuses. The *Four Absolutes* were a constant in our lives growing up, and I'm grateful for that invaluable grounding. Yet, as you know, I was never able to jump into the cause with both feet as you did. Nor did I ever get comfortable sharing with you the reasons for my resistance. So I will try to now.

You'll remember that, as a young woman, on separate occasions I visited MRA's two largest centres in the US—its headquarters on Mackinac Island, Michigan, and *The Club* in Los Angeles. In both instances, I felt as though I'd been thrown to the wolves, and the pack had been programmed to attack. Accusations that I was leading an immoral life, from strangers who did not know my life, did not sit well. In my mind, the friendships that I had—both sexes—were normal and healthy. The school dances that we all attended together did not make us sinners, and the lipstick that I wore did not make me a tart. The accusations made by the MRA followers never seemed to correlate with its philosophy of *absolute* love. Just as troubling, though, Dad, was my concept of the unusual control at the top.

I never met Frank Buchman, MRA's founder and leader, but from my vantage, his followers seemed to worship him to the extreme, and he, in turn, appeared to impose excessive control over them—a circumstance that gave the movement a cultlike feel. And it made me uneasy. The group rituals where members publicly shared guidance from God, and confessed their sins, felt almost programmed at times, and that further added to my uneasiness. It just wasn't for me.

In the end, Dad, in spite of my resistance to MRA, I am ready to accept that, through its teachings, you gave us a morally sound home to grow up in, and what greater gift is that? I agree with Don, who, in spite of his aversion to MRA—and his professed atheism—once expressed his pride in you for your foresight into its vision for the world, and your willingness to commit yourself to a cause that you believed in. To his thought, I'll add a final one of my own: I fully believe that, had MRA never entered your world, the goodness of your wonderful King family would have prevailed. You all travelled the high road, lighting the path for those of us to follow. We could not lose our way.

OK, that's really it for now! Time to drop Mother a line … maybe two.

Sure missing you, Dad! I love you,
El

Mother
Ruby Loan Hall Anderson King

Born December 1, 1902—Montreal, Quebec, Canada
Died September 27, 1985—Calgary, Alberta, Canada

Dear Mother,

I sat with you around the clock for two days at Bethany Care Centre before you died in the wee hours of that chilly September morning. You had been a resident at Bethany for the previous two years. You had suffered from bipolar disorder for at least thirty years—probably longer—and things started to go sideways when you could no longer tolerate the medications required to temper it. Then you developed multiple myeloma, and that was the beginning of the end.

Your hand was becoming cold and clammy as death summoned, yet it was only warmth that I felt as I thought back on the wise and wonderful mother that I'd been blessed to have. A mother who listened and loved ... unconditionally.

After a final goodbye kiss, I walked from Bethany with tears streaming down my cheeks. It was still pitch dark as I reached my car, and, as I slid behind the wheel, I unexpectedly burst into wracking sobs. They never let up for the entire ride home. The sudden sobs surprised me, yet I instinctively knew that they weren't because of your death, they were about your life—tears for all the years you suffered with a hellish mental illness, hell enough by itself, but compounded by the disquieting certainty that few people understood it, or wanted to. It was that resounding truth that was breaking my heart. How many in our own small sphere still held the notion that all you needed to do was *pull up your socks*? I knew that I had to forgive, that bipolar disease is difficult to understand, and at the outset, we all struggled with it. I'm not sure whether you ever fully grasped it yourself.

When you were first diagnosed years ago, the condition was called manic-depression, which is more definitive. In the early days, we (the immediate family) would see you plunge into a depression, a state in which it was abundantly evident that you were suffering. When the depression lifted, we rejoiced that you were better. I haven't forgotten the day that Don (your astute son) said to me, "I'm starting to think that when Mother's depressions lift, we're fooled into thinking she's well. What we're actually seeing is the other side of the coin." As your disease progressed, it became ever more evident that he was right, although you were never able to recognize it yourself. You only knew that, after weeks existing under a crushing low, slipping into a high was sheer bliss. You felt like a million bucks. Early on, even your doctors were slow to recognize that these highs were as abnormal as the lows—that you had no control over either phase. It goes without saying that they were therefore ill-equipped to treat both phases with any degree of success. And by the way, are you aware that I never heard you actually voice the word *depressed*? You always expressed it as *fatigue*. I could find you in a paralyzing black hole, and you would say, "I'm so tired, dear."

When I got home from Bethany that morning, I crawled into bed to catch a few zzz before taking on the day, but exhausted as I was, I could not sleep. I kept ruminating over the thought that yours was a life that never got lived. Never quite got off the ground. You were a dedicated homemaker, and good at it, but I was never sure whether you were overjoyed with this role. I wanted to bring you back, sweep away the depressions, and fling open the door for you to take another crack at life. What would that have looked like for you? What would have turned your crank? Did you harbour a secret desire that you never communicated? I wish I'd asked you those questions.

You had earned a teaching diploma at Normal School, but you did confess that you hadn't really taken to teaching. So I assume that wouldn't make the list. I do remember how animated you were when talking about your first job doing clerical work for Mr. Ferguson's insurance company. You spoke so fondly of *Fergie* and the office gang. It was a happy time and place for you. Did you long for the stimulation and companionship of the old office gang? I'm sure many women of your generation, confined to the home, suffered in silence. So much was expected of you, so little appreciation in return.

Many psychiatrists, when seeking to explain the root cause of depression, favour the idea that it's suppressed anger. In the absence of anything obvious leading me in that direction, I'm not inclined to pursue that premise in your case, especially since it was not a theory held by Dr. Roxborough, your smart—and exceptionally caring—psychiatrist. He viewed your illness as purely a chemical imbalance, and directed his treatment accordingly. You often had sudden, seemingly unprovoked mood changes that supported his theory, but I will always believe that other factors contribute—life changes, fear, anxiety, grief. Sometimes I questioned whether the expectations placed on you by *Moral Re-Armament* played a role. Was it always your choice to participate, or were you pressured by Dad? And you will remember how you plunged into depression without fail every Christmas, presumably in response to its demands. Then I have to ask, did the anxiety of the Christmas season alter your brain chemistry? Maybe that will always be a mystery.

One thing I have done is a lot of reading by, or about, others who suffered similar disorders as you. You were in notable company—Art Buchwald, Dick Cavett, Winston Churchill, Patty Duke, Glenn Gould, Vivien Leigh, Isaac Newton, Jackson Pollock.... Don't you wish we could make a pot of tea and invite these good people over for a cup and a chat? It would be an embracing and empathetic circle for sure.

Patty Duke's book, *A Brilliant Madness*, is an unflinching *coming out* about her life with manic-depressive disease. She speaks openly about years of chaos before diagnosis, and the long struggle to find peace through treatment. Her disclosure is also a direct attempt to erase the stigma of the disease, which is beyond brave in her artificial world of Hollywood, and its unrealistic demands. Hers is a compassionate story, addressing every aspect of the disease, including interesting thoughts of its possible cause. One view that rings true for me is that of a former president of the American Psychiatric Association, who labelled it a *bio-psychosocial disorder*, suggesting that a genetic predisposition likely sets the stage, then life stressors alter the body chemistry. The one word that crops up with greatest frequency amongst those describing the disorder is *elusive*.

Margaret Trudeau, wife of Pierre Trudeau, our former prime minister (and mother of our current prime minister), wrote a touching story, *Changing My Mind*. *Maggie* says that puzzling mood fluctuations, which neither she nor her family understood, began in childhood. Reading this part of her story made me wonder whether your symptoms began years before any of us recognized that something might be wrong. What do you think? I do remember your daily naps throughout my childhood, which really weren't naps at all—they were two-hour sleeps. It seemed normal to me then, just part of your routine, but now I wonder whether those overlong siestas were an escape from depression. Can you imagine poor Margaret Trudeau dealing with this monstrous affliction on the world stage? I confess I had no idea what was behind her offbeat behaviour. Canadians just thought she must be *on something*. Bless her heart, she, like Patty Duke, shares her story to help other sufferers.

William Styron's memoir, *Darkness Visible*, takes my breath away. His portrayal of the depressions he suffered—"dark joylessness, inexplicable agony, fogbound horror, hell's black depths"—are profound, especially when in the same breath he calls it "a disorder so painful and elusive that it verges close to being beyond description." I think he, more than anyone, brings it home to me how deeply you suffered. I agonize that we were unable to do more to ease your pain. I am so sorry.

Well, that's all behind us now, and I want to assure you that when my thoughts turn to you today, which is often, your illness doesn't dominate. It's our home in Scarboro that takes centre stage, the warm, safe place where you were always there to greet me and I was always happy to come home. And what a wonderful neighbourhood to grow up in—the epitome of the saying, "It takes a village to raise a child." We had our very own village, safe and secure, where families moved in and stayed. I went through twelve years of school with the same group of friends, and, now in our eighties, we're still friends. It makes me think of you and Blanche, your childhood friend. I never saw you more joyful than when you were with Blanche. I can still see the two of you laughing your heads off together. I wish you had gotten together more often. Blanche was so good for you.

I return to Scarboro now and then for a sentimental walkabout to re-live happy times growing up in the neighbourhood. Scarboro was planned and developed so beautifully, with its lovely curved roads, attractive shrubs and trees, ornamental parks, and beautiful boulevards running between the sidewalks and the road. I miss those boulevards when I walk in my current neighbourhood, where the sidewalks slope with each driveway—hazardous in winter, and an enemy for aged hips and knees any time of year. The boulevards accommodated the driveway slopes, allowing the adjacent sidewalks to run flat. Not only that, there were sidewalks on *both* sides of the street. When did the city stop doing that?

On my Scarboro walkabouts, I find changes to the old neighbourhood that I'm not crazy about. Would you believe they've sealed off most of the streets bordering 17th Avenue! It means you can't get in or out of the neighbourhood by car without advance planning. And when you finally make it in, you won't believe the yield and stop signs all over the place; there was no need for a single sign when I was first behind the wheel. And remember the streetlight in the centre of the road up by Aunt Lil's house? Where my gang used to hang out when our evening's activities were over, and it was time to go home, but we didn't want to? Well, guess what they've done with our meeting place? They've turned it into a traffic circle. A *traffic* circle! There's traffic there? What on earth? Where do they expect the neighbourhood kids to loiter after curfew now?

And don't get me started on the old character homes that have been pulverized and replaced with big boxes that don't fit the flavour of the neighbourhood. Or the additions to homes—ours for one—that have eaten up their beautiful backyards. Where do families play croquet on a Sunday afternoon? Still, after all my complaining, there's something about the neighbourhood that has always drawn me back, and in fact, the pull was so strong twenty years ago that I wrote a book about it. I told Dad about the book in a recent letter to him, but I've saved most of my post-publication news for you.

The book tells the story of my years growing up in Calgary—the '40s and '50s—indisputably the best time and place to be a kid. The book is called *The House With The Light On*, referring to our home on Scarboro Avenue and the front door light you always left on until I was safely in for the night. I swear it was the only house in the whole neighbourhood with its light on whenever a guy delivered me home from a date. Surely I wasn't always the last one on the block to come home. I haven't forgotten a favourite saying of yours: "If you're the last one to leave the party, you've stayed too long."

I published *The House With The Light On* when I was sixty-six years old, an age when you'd expect that I'd have given thought to a marketing plan. But the embarrassing truth is, I hadn't. Nor had I held any expectation for its success. So I stumbled along, and with the generous support of local independent booksellers, the book eventually assumed the job of marketing itself. It found a niche, especially amongst Calgary's old guard. The aftermath has been a joy ride that I can't wait to tell you about. The story began the first day the book hit the shelves.

I picked up the phone to a voice with a soft Irish lilt asking, "Are you the author of *The House With The Light On*?" "Yes, I am," I replied. "May I ask who's calling?" That's when the soft Irish lilt erupted into an ear-splitting shriek: "It's her! It's her!" And in the background cries of excitement escalated into high-pitched squeals: "Really, Mom? Are you sure?" Finally the breathless caller gathered her composure and asked, "Is *The House* referred to in the title located at 319 Scarboro Avenue?"

"Why, yes," I replied. "You've read the book already?"

"No, I haven't," she said, "but my family is living in your house."

And that was the beginning of a whole new chapter.

Patricia's day began with an alert from a neighbour who'd been lazily scanning the morning newspaper over a second cuppa. Having lived in the community for many years, an article recounting the book launch of a local author's memoir piqued the neighbour's interest. She grabbed her phone: "Patricia, have you read the article on page B11 of this morning's paper?" she asked. "You haven't? Go get your paper right now. I think the house featured might be yours. The author's name is King, and I know that a King family lived in your house years ago. Go look now. G'bye!"

Patricia rummaged through the paper feverishly until she found page B11. Her eyes darted about the article, but found no connection between her address and that of *The House With The Light On*. She backed up to the beginning and worked her way through again, this time with care, line by line. Still no hint that the book title had anything to do with her house. She did, however, believe in the stars, and the stars were telling her that her friend's instincts were right. And since the article conveniently published the author's phone number, she picked up the phone. And that's how I met the affable Patricia, now living in our old home. She quickly extended a warm invitation to come for coffee, which I readily accepted … with a measure of curiosity. We settled on a date and time, and ended the call. One minute later, the phone rang again: "Oh, I forgot," said Patricia, "please bring seven copies of your book for my family in Ireland." So, Mother, I went back home, carrying seven books.

Patricia, an attractive brunette with a peaches and cream complexion, greeted me at our old front door on a sunny August morning. She was bursting with enthusiasm and brimming with stories she couldn't wait to tell. Diane and grandson, Andrew, age eight, accompanied me on the visit. Diane had never seen the interior of this house, and Andrew, a budding artist and historian, was especially keen to see the setting of all the stories he'd heard Grandma tell about her childhood: "When I was your age …" It warms my heart to see that Andrew is as happy a kid as I was at his age.

Patricia waved us inside, and at first glance, everything was just as I remembered it—the light fixtures overhead and down the hall, on my left, the inviting living room closed off by glass doors, and to the right, the staircase with its wooden railing supported by iron spindles, rising above the steam radiator. Everything had remained faithful to the home's 1912 architecture. I had come home. Then we stepped into the kitchen—tile floors, granite countertops, stainless steel appliances, and spreading beyond—spilling into the backyard—a large family room, half bathroom, and laundry room. Where was I?

You talked about a main-floor bathroom forever, but we insensitively dismissed you, didn't we? Apart from the fact that we saw no possible way to squeeze one into the limited square footage of the main floor, running upstairs to the bathroom wasn't a problem for us. No big deal for young, strong legs. Except Dad developed Parkinson's Disease after we all left home, and it became a big deal, didn't it? That's when you got serious about a solution for a main floor bathroom … except you still couldn't squeeze it in. So you moved to a bungalow in Scarboro Heights.

Patricia sat us at the kitchen table with coffee, milk and cookies, impatient to tell us the story of how she found the house. Her opening words revealed a superstitious bent that would crop up a few more times during our visit. "My family moved to Calgary from Ireland in 1998," she began, "then returned home for a year, before coming back for good. A colleague of my husband's (a psychiatrist) suggested we explore the Scarboro neighbourhood as a possible place to settle. So, I was driving down Scarboro Avenue trying to get a feel for the area, when a black cat suddenly flew out from the side of the road, crossing directly in front of my car. As I braked to avoid hitting it, I watched it run up a driveway.

When I craned to see where it went, I spotted a FOR SALE sign almost hidden from the street. I would have missed the sign had it not been for the cat." Viewing the black cat as an omen, Patricia pulled up to the curb. Without hesitation, she approached the house, climbing the front steps and ringing the doorbell. The owner answered, and invited her in. After taking her on a cursory walk-through, they entered a discussion of price. Two minutes later, Patricia phoned her husband from the front steps. "Kevin," she said, " I've just bought us a house!"

Following this introductory story—and the cookies and milk—Patricia introduced us to the members of her family that were making the house a home—three darling daughters—Alexandra, Victoria, and Claudia—and their three pets—Nikita the hamster, Tallulah the Mexican Chihuahua, and Tessa, a grey, long-haired cat. Then she was ready to take us on the full tour.

Prominently featured throughout the house were icons of the Virgin Mary, surrounded by a profusion of girlish adornments, effects never seen in this setting when we lived there. After a walk-through of the main floor—the old and the new—Patricia escorted us upstairs.

Your bedroom at the front was now swathed in pink lace, and occupied by Alexandra. Was it always that small? How did you get your bulky antique furniture in there? I do remember your dresser sitting at a bit of an awkward angle to avoid blocking the window. And I never heard you complain about your pint-sized closet—its two small opposing racks managed your and Dad's frugal wardrobes just fine. Both racks were now jam-packed with Alexandra's beautiful collection. Then it was on to Victoria's bedroom in the middle, where I announced, "This was my room." Without skipping a beat, Patricia whirled around and said, "You're a Virgo then." "How did you know?"

I asked, incredulously. "Because Victoria's a Virgo," she replied with a matter-of-fact shrug. *Ah*, I said under my breath, *I never knew this was the Virgo room*. Claudia occupied Stan and Don's room, although her canopied four-poster bed and Taj Mahal draperies were a far cry from the cream-coloured metal beds the boys slept in, with the green and taupe checked spreads you made for them. Beyond Claudia's room was the new fabulous master suite—with full ensuite—built over the addition to the kitchen below. You're rolling your eyes, aren't you? So am I, but for a different reason. You're thinking: *Two full bathrooms on the same floor? Such extravagance.* While I'm thinking: *Sacrificing a croquet court for a few extra square feet of house? That borders on sacrilege.* That beautiful backyard in summer was one of the house's most compelling features, wouldn't you agree?

Finally, Patricia ushered us back down and outside. Oh, Mother, more big changes. Our wonderful long driveway that ran the full length of the property had been decommissioned to accommodate two more additions jutting out the side of the house. This meant the garage doors had to be relocated to open into the alley. Gone was the mile of snow shovelling in the winter, but gone, too, was my roller skating rink and my hopscotch court. And so much for hitting tennis balls against the garage. I suppose the inside was improved, but the outside sure wasn't the kid-friendly place I knew. Well, there was one exception: they'd erected a spectacular treehouse straight out of Disney World in the big tree in the southeast corner of the backyard. If I'd had that beauty when I was a kid, I would have packed up and moved in. My needs would have been few—a blanket and pillow, my favourite book, a flashlight, and my teddy bear. Breakfast delivered would have been nice, as would have having Helen and Jean for lunch every day—peanut butter and banana sandwiches. But since that wasn't to be, I packed my dreams, and climbed the stairs to the present-day treehouse with Diane and Andrew. Patricia had given me advance notice of its housewarming party to come, but since we would not be able to attend, Andrew brought an early gift: a paper lantern—his idea for Alexandra, Victoria, and Claudia to have their own *house with a light on*.

We ended the visit with Patricia taking us down the narrow, seldom-used east side of the house, where she stopped and pointed to the dining room window, casually saying, "You probably know the woman who appears in the window from time to time," calmly adding, "I don't think it's the same person that turns up in the rumpus room occasionally, do you?" What could I say, except, "I doubt it's the same person!" Mother, you didn't tell me that we had ghosts! For sure Dad didn't know, or he'd have turned himself inside out conjuring up a weekly ghost story.

The following December, Dick and I received a written invitation from Patricia and Kevin to their annual Christmas party, which they noted would largely be attended by neighbours. We accepted. But as party night rolled around, I found myself resisting the event without really knowing why. I had an awful time getting myself presentable for the occasion, and poor Dick had his hands full getting me out the door. I was a silent partner for the drive across the city.

We found our old house ablaze with Christmas lights. "We had a single wreath hanging in the living room window," I gasped. "It had a candle in the middle. That was it for our decorations." The memory brought me back to Cousin Audrey's description of her household's lone adornment—the same conventional wreath in the window. "But ours had a flashing candle," she boasted, grinning smugly. "I used to stand in the dark, and twist the bulb off and on."

From the moment we rang the front doorbell, I knew that coming had been a mistake. Family Christmases in this home were the best in the world: the eight-foot tree in the corner by the window, decorated by Stan and Don and me (under Don's command); your uncomplicated but heavenly turkey dinners; Aunt Mildred's second-to-none fruit pudding (steamed in a Nabob coffee can); inventive games with the aunts, uncles, and cousins; and a lone wreath hanging majestically in the front window. Not flashing.

Now I am stepping into a home of excess, where extravagant decorations dripped from everywhere. Strangers huddled in comfortable cliques, showing little interest in a lost soul from another time. Who were these people? What were they doing in *my* house? Why weren't they playing games? Charades. Twenty Questions. And what was the tree doing in *that* corner? It's always been to the right of the front window. With a pit in my stomach, I nibbled a few hors d'oeuvres, out of respect for Patricia's sumptuous spread, then the moment I reasoned we could exit without insulting our gracious hosts, I grabbed Dick and made for the door. I couldn't wait to get home … to the Christmas decoration that holds a place of honour in our house—a choirboy that Stephen made for me back in grade school using folded pages of a *Reader's Digest* magazine. Its Styrofoam head holds two lopsided eyes, a crooked mouth, no nose, and three uneven strands of yellow wool for his hair. I can hear that choirboy sing.

My initial journey back home in the summer was nostalgic, and at times amusing, but my return at Christmas was unsettling. This time, I could not relate to this place as home. But then, it wasn't home. I was in a house filled with excess—*two* more bathrooms, more furnishings, more toys, more decorations, more everything. The modest, homey home that I knew and loved, the one that had no need for *more* because it had *enough*, was gone. Then one day I read a quote by Sam Ewing that spoke to me: "When you finally go back to your old home, you find it wasn't the old home you missed, but your childhood." That, too, Mr. Ewing, but I still missed the old home.

Now, back to the book ... David Bly, heritage columnist for the *Calgary Herald* at the time, came to my book launch. At the close of the evening, we talked about expectations, and David expressed a concern he had that new writers expect to get rich. I assured him that I held no such presumption, that I'd consider it a victory if I broke even. What I hadn't banked on, though, was the flood of phone calls and letters from readers that would deliver riches beyond measure. As I re-read their letters, I am getting to know all these wonderful people again. I'll share some with you, so that you can get to know them, too.

It was especially rewarding to hear from non-Calgarians who anticipated little connection to the story, then discovered a tale of the times that triggered memories of their own lives during the same period in their respective cities. "This could have been my story growing up in Winnipeg," wrote one woman. "I even went to CGIT on the same night of the week—Tuesday." Linda, a Newfoundland woman I met while travelling in South Africa, wrote, "*The House With The Light On* was a joy to read. We are the same age, and had much in common. Even the title could have applied to our house." A total stranger from Saskatchewan added her postscript to the title—"My parents left the light on, too—and flashed it on and off if I stayed outside too long!" Annie wrote from Didsbury: "Your childhood and youth were very different from mine, but there's something pretty universal about knowing the deep-down love that exists between family members." And all the way from *down under*, Jacki had this to say: "Growing up in Calgary has so many similarities to growing up in Melbourne—no wonder Australians feel so at home in Canada."

The majority of my readers, though, have been long-time Calgary residents, eager to relive shared memories of people, places, and events with me. The first such letter arrived within a week of publication. The writer's excitement was palpable as she listed—at length—all the people and places we had in common. Except her spirits sagged with her unapologetic closing line: "But you forgot to mention the *Dilly Dilly Ice Cream Parlour*." She would not be the first to point out an omission such as this, passed over because it had simply not been part of my experience. But I was aghast when I discovered the unthinkable omission of a setting that should have received top billing in my book. I'll never forgive myself.

Peggy wrote, "My mother owned *Scarboro Confectionary* on 17th Avenue." Yes, of course! Except we never called it *Scarboro Confectionary*, it was *George's* to us. Now I'm learning that it wasn't *George* who owned it, but Peggy's mother. So who was *George* anyway? All I can say is that Peggy's mother's confectionary was the setting for some of my happiest memories. It's where I'd take my allowance to splurge on penny candy—"I'd like two cents' worth of jawbreakers, please, and three cents' worth of those … oh, how much is that all-day sucker?" I can still feel my pack of friends wedged beside me in the store's close quarters, jostling for position at the candy counter, fingers smudging the glass as we pointed to our desired sweet. Inevitably, pennies would slip from our grasp, and decorate the muddy floor below the counter. "Helen, you're stepping on my money!" The patience of the beautiful people bagging our requests—two of this and three of that—day after day, is beyond imagining. They were saints.

At least once a week, Dad would have a hankering for some ice cream for dessert. "El, how would you like to ride your bike to *George's* for a brick," he'd say. You'll remember that the minuscule freezer compartment of our fridge was permanently packed with frost, leaving no room to store ice cream or anything else. Well, there was one exception: at some point a tray of ice cubes got wedged in there, but the cubes never saw the light of day, because no one could chisel them out. In any event, I loved being assigned the ice cream run because it got me out of clearing the dishes. Plus, ice cream was a welcome departure from your usual healthy desserts of canned fruit. When I got back from *George's*, you had the unenviable assignment of cutting one small brick into five equal portions. If I recall, you solved the task by slicing a sliver from one end for yourself, then cutting the rest into four perfect quarters. Easy.

Other readers challenged my historic accuracy: Ralph called to take issue with my story of Brother Don following the bus up 7th Street into Mount Royal when he was a little kid. "I doubt the bus went up 7th Street," he said, "it more likely went up 8th." Well, Ralph, 8th is definitely more of a thoroughfare, but Don remembers following the bus as it ran past our house, and the house was on 7th.

I especially love Cousin Rich's story of arriving at the *Winter Club* one morning for his men's tennis league, and a friend greeting him with: "I've just read a new book called *The House With The Light On*. Have you heard of it? You grew up in Calgary, didn't you? You'd love it." "As a matter of fact, I have read it," Rich deadpanned, adding, "By the way, what did you think of the 'Ritchie' character in the story?" Rascal as a kid. Still a rascal.

Readers of every age and walk of life came out of the woodwork, wanting to say hello and share connections, whether tangible or tenuous: "I was a long-time friend of your father's." "My father worked at the Robin Hood Flour Mill." "I used to usher at the Palace Theatre." "My family lived on Superior Avenue, across the alley from you." "My mother went to Central High with you." "Marilyn sent me a copy of your book... ." "Shirley sent me a copy of your book... ." "I lent your book to someone—I can't remember who—and it never came back. Please send another." Some wrote full updates of family members that I knew as a kid. I loved that. Then, you won't believe what happened next!

One day, Denis, the adorable little tyke who lived down the street growing up, stepped back into my life. Remember him? I'd understand if you didn't because I scarcely knew him back then myself. He was the youngest of seven—the Catholic family on the corner. He was not only considerably younger than me, but the division was compounded by the lines drawn between Catholics and Protestants. Wasn't it a shame that we never got to know the Catholic kids? Well, five decades later, the curly-haired, five-year-old had morphed into a handsome, middle-aged man standing on my doorstep, eager to connect. We'd both moved across town and were once again neighbours. Denis had read *The House With The Light On,* and wanted to reminisce. Discrepancy in age and religious affiliation had evaporated.

After chewing the fat about the good old days in Scarboro, Denis left with another copy of the book to deliver to his sister, his family's firstborn, gravely ill in hospital. Soon after, he lost that sister, and the second in line readily took up the family mantle. Maureen, outgoing, capable, and big-hearted, is loved by all who meet her, and especially adored by her younger siblings, who are thriving in the warmth of her embrace. When she read the book, she was not content to just celebrate the past, she wanted to write her own afterword, by gathering fellow Scarboro residents from the past to meet for lunch—pizza and nostalgia.

The first such gathering took place at *Boston Pizza* in October 2010, and it's been an annual event ever since. Our collection of men and women up to thirty strong, ages seventy and up—Catholics, Protestants, Jews—invade the restaurant en masse every October to remember and laugh. We hobble in with an inventory of aches and pains standard for our age group, and, three hours later, strut out the door like a pack of teen-agers on uppers. Old friends are new again … and young again.

The McGraths: L to R, Maureen, Denis, Patricia

But now I have to return to Denis as a five-year-old, and my favourite story of him. As you know, Aunt Lil lived across the street from Denis, and she also ran a kindergarten class in our church's basement down the street. Denis was not enrolled in her kindergarten, but that didn't stop him from showing up. Every morning, as Aunt Lil was making preparations to begin the day, she'd look up to see Denis outside the window, with his nose pressed against the glass. She didn't have the heart to leave him in the cold alone, so she'd wave him inside. It soon became a routine: Denis with his nose on the window, Aunt Lil waving him inside … until the day he took for granted that he no longer had to do the nose-on-the-glass routine—he could come in directly like all the other kids, and take his place as a full-fledged member of the class. Aunt Lil, on the other hand, now faced a problem. When it was time to prepare her monthly billing statements, she had to address the matter of Denis, who was now attending as regularly as her paying students. And so, she popped a bill into the mailbox of Denis's parents across the street, which is how they learned that Denis was even attending kindergarten, let alone one housed in the basement of a *Protestant* church! But since he loved Mrs. King, and she loved him, they paid, and he stayed.

So, you can see, Mother, the aftermath of this book has been a regular odyssey. After my early encounter with Denis, more heartwarming stories surrounding the neighbourhood started coming out of the woodwork. I have welcomed all connections with readers, whether by letter, phone, or face to face. I'm touched when someone finds enjoyment through a shared childhood experience.

Carl, whose parents built their home on Sunderland Avenue in 1930, called, bursting with excitement. He came for coffee carrying photos and a supply of *Vistas*, the Sunalta

School yearbook. He said that his mother stayed in the Scarboro home for sixty-one years. Dick, a fellow member of our church, approached me after the service one Sunday with a hearty laugh: "Loved your book," he said, "and all this time I thought I was the only kid who ever slid down the flour chute into the Fourex Bakery!" (I never told you I did that, did I?) Alex, a fellow member of our golf club, approached me one day, keen to share his memory of renting ponies as a kid at the Ovans Stables as I had done. We nodded in assent at the vision of those stubborn little Shetlands with minds of their own. Through a good old belly laugh, Alex reminded me that, "The only decent pony was Diamond. Daisy and Mabel were terrible!" I never knew the Ovans ponies even had names. It's clear to me now that Mr. Ovans plunked me on either Daisy or Mabel every time, because I never got either one to budge beyond the alley leading from the stable. Alex must've been the kid galloping past me, heading for the coulee … on Diamond.

Pure joy was evident in the voices of Mr. and Mrs. Hawryluk, calling on extension phones to laugh together with me over shared memories. Mrs. Hawryluk, recalling my episode getting buried in the heap of sawdust at Cushing Mills, was keen to relate her experiences at the same mills. Noting my displeasure over having impossibly curly hair when I dreamed of a straight, sleek look, she chuckled at her memory of the opposite—she suffered bone straight hair, and longed for curls. But she found an ingenious solution to her dilemma. She would hike down to Cushing Mills, gather up the curly wood shavings from their yard, and pin them onto the ends of her hair. Voila—her own brand of extensions! She and I agreed that the one trait we had in common with all young girls of the time, was wanting what we didn't have.

Unforeseen bonuses of writing the book came in the form of invitations to book clubs, senior clubs, and church and school events. An especially memorable evening began with an invitation to join our beloved Scarboro United Church's senior potluck supper, with a request to "be prepared to do a reading from your book." I selected an anecdote I'd written of Marilyn Perkins, longstanding musical director and stalwart of the church. Everyone present at the supper knew and loved Marilyn. Sadly, she had passed away only months before this particular evening, and in spite of the fact that we all still grieved for her, laughter naturally accompanied thoughts of her—she had a wicked sense of humour.

My chosen passage described the day when I was a member of her junior choir long years before, and rascal that I was, I decided to put Marilyn to the test. From my position in the back row, I tried getting away with moving my lips and not singing. I should have known better—Marilyn's highly trained ear could pluck out individual voices (or absence thereof) within the first bar. Without skipping a beat, she stretched onto her tiptoes to catch my eye, and called out, "Eleanor, don't just move your lips. Sing!" Outed! Bob, a delightful senior in attendance, laughed uproariously at this story, then added one of his own: He'd joined one of Marilyn's choirs for the sheer joy of being part of her group. In spite of their warm friendship, Marilyn couldn't help cringing at the distraction of his off-key vocals. Finally one day she took him aside after practice, and laughingly whispered, "Bob, why don't you just move your lips."

Then, one sunny January day, I found myself surrounded by the opposite age group, at the opposite corner of the neighbourhood—in my beloved Sunalta School. I was greeted by eye-catching artwork covering the walls in the hallways and stairwells, in stark contrast to the sterile common areas in my day. When climbing the stairs to the second floor, my feet found familiar depressions in each slate step, though each was deeper now—footprints of time. I was the honoured guest of a class of Grade 3 would-be writers. Jackson, their composed and professional spokesman, introduced me to his mates, announcing that their assignment for the day was to interview an author for *Youthinkit Magazine*, a local publication by, and for, youth. Brock, a volunteer dad, sat in. I noted how fortunate Jackson and his classmates were to have a volunteer dad in their midst. During my nine years attending Sunalta School, no dad ever made an appearance. If a parent showed up at all, it was a mom.

We talked about other changes in the school and in the neighbourhood, the most startling for me being the coulee directly behind the school where I spent hours playing with my friends, summer and winter. The children were mystified by the playground I described. "How could that be ? Crowchild Trail runs through there. How come you didn't get run over?"

Jackson then explained that the class's assignment didn't stop with the interview—they were to write an article about the author, and adapt it for suitability in the morning newspaper. Wait a minute. Grade *3*? I thought back to myself in Grade 3—Miss Allison's class—when I could not conceive of writing a composition of any description, never mind interview an adult, and tailor the resulting article to meet newspaper guidelines. As I was trying to comprehend all this, Jackson grinned impishly, and brought me fully into the world of today's eight-year-old with a confession: "Actually, Mrs. Byers," he said, "we didn't really have to interview you at all. We already Googled you!" (Yes, Mother, I've promised to explain the technology of using the search engine "Google" on a computer to find information on everything under the sun. Be patient.)

Then Jackson took me on a tour of the whole school. I wondered how I could possibly impress a young man who was mature beyond his years. But he was pretty bowled over when I named every last teacher I'd had, and the grade they taught, while pointing out their respective classrooms. When we reached our final stop—the big, beautiful library—I said, "Jackson, you won't believe this, but I used to play basketball in here." Jackson was speechless. Basketball in the library? "We're standing in my old gymnasium," I said. "We didn't have a big auditorium like you have. And our library was so small I can't even remember where it was." Jackson stared at me in disbelief—a school without an auditorium? Unthinkable. I explained that his auditorium was added in 1958, six years after I left the school. "But," I assured him, "we managed physical education classes just fine in this library!"

Two other occasions brought me back to the school. The first time was for the ribbon-cutting of the fabulous new murals, commissioned by the parents' fundraising group, on the exterior walls of the auditorium by artist Dean Stanton—friendly faces waving to the passing motorists on Crowchild Trail. The second visit was for the christening of elaborate new playground equipment, also funded by the parents' group. When chatting with the woman heading up this group, I made the comment that no such parents' group existed when I was a child. "Oh, but back then," she said, "your parents had so much more money than we have." Hello? Mother, you never told me. Where were you hiding it? In coffee cans under the bed?

As you know, Aunt Lil was a fan of book clubs, so it would please her no end to know that many such clubs flourish in Scarboro. Two made my book their selection of the month and invited me to join their members for discussion. The first invitation came from Sharon in November 2006: "We're meeting this month at 420 Scarboro Avenue," she said. "Will you be needing directions or a ride?"

"No," I gasped, scarcely believing my ears. "I can find that address."

I have written Aunt Lil about that evening in her home, where I found it as unsettling as the Christmas party at our old home. I wanted to find everything as I remembered it. Because it was perfect. I guess Sam Ewing was right—it's my childhood that I miss.

The second Scarboro book club was held in the Weavers' old address on Superior Avenue, a house you'll also remember. I knew it well, but I'd never been inside, so I entered with no pre-conceived visions to throw me off balance. I was free to enjoy the warmth of the home and the circle of women within. The women in this club were full of questions, and especially eager to learn about past residents of the neighbourhood, particularly the owners of their respective homes. Many had already researched the history of their homes, but welcomed personal stories from the kid who lived there fifty years before. It was heartwarming to witness this current generation of women, committed to preserving the past for the generations to follow. Scarboro is in good hands.

I was the guest of honour at many more book clubs, but I have to tell you about one that particularly made me think of you. Members of this club were all school teachers, and they named their club W.I.N.E., an acronym for Women Interested in Novels and Enlightenment. The centrepiece of their evening was a full dinner featuring wine, an event where they gathered their thoughts for serious book discussion to follow. They were enthusiastic readers, and their lively exchange of views even included marketing strategies for me. And would you believe, Doreen, the detail-oriented hostess, had planted sheet music on her piano for a piece that I had named as one I had performed as a child. Remember Mrs. Walker's annual concerts? (Thank goodness Doreen didn't ask me to play it again.) Club members then took turns describing their particular connections to my book through personal stories. And they brought school memorabilia and photos to enhance their stories. But, as entertaining as her club members were, Doreen still won the day when she broke into song:

> *Oh, your Jenkins store is the place to go,*
> *Where the quality's high and the price is low,*
> *Get the best for less and save your dough,*
> *They are waiting to serve you at Jenkins.*

The *Jenkins Jingle*! Remember that, Mother? You phoned *Jenkins* every Saturday for our food supply, and your order—packed in boxes—would be delivered to our side door later the same day. The rest of the weekend, we'd hear the *Jenkins Jingle* played repeatedly on the radio—"Oh, your *Jenkins* store is the place to go...." "How on earth did you remember that?" I asked Doreen in disbelief. "Because I wrote it," she replied, laughing so hard she nearly fell off her chair. When she gathered her composure, she explained: "*Jenkins* opened a contest for an advertising jingle, offering a prize for the winner. So I got to work, wrote one, and submitted it. And I won!" I was so dumbstruck with her story, I can't remember if she told us what her prize was. The evening, though, was priceless—it went on till 12:45 a.m.

A favourite letter came from Ken Penley, son of the people who owned *Penley's Dance Academy*, where you and Dad hung out during your courting days. Seems to me you had two choices—the movies or Penley's, right? Ken was eighty-four when he wrote to tell me of his connections to people and places that he found in my book. His casual style of listing items brought a kind of eloquence to his letter of May 3, 2005:

'Thank you for your kind reference to *Penley's Dancing Academy*—my parents'.

Mart Kenney is still living, in his nineties. I write to him.

My parents often had dinner at the *Tea Kettle Inn*; I had tea there.

I remember the Hull's house. I delivered parcels for *McGill Drug* and left them with that gardener.

My son had Cy Groves as a teacher. Invited him to a sail at Chestermere. The wind came up and Groves accused him of trying to drown him!

I attended Connaught. Sunalta was an opponent at track meets at Mewata. I was lucky to win the last event to break a tie. Sorry.

I bought records, too. Seventy-eights. I got mine at the *Bay*, where, on Saturday morning, poor sellers sold for ten cents. I like old jazz and picked up several for dimes.

I went to the *Kinema Theatre* often. One day I saw a typed message on the screen saying, "Ken Penley, go home."

I regret never meeting Ken face to face, but I got to know him through reciprocating letters. When I spotted his obituary in the *Calgary Herald* on April 18, 2014, I shed a tear. I had lost a good friend.

I learned something about character from a kind, gentle man who had a tough start in life. You'll remember the kids from Lowery Gardens who went to Sunalta School with me, their families squatting in shacks down by the river north of the school. The uncomfortable truth is that their poverty separated *them from us*, and I can only hope that we Scarboro kids were not insensitive or unkind. My heart stopped the day I received a letter dated January 7, 2020, which began: "A couple of days ago I finished reading your 2003 memoir, and I am compelled to let you know I enjoyed it very much. I was one of the Lowery Gardens kids who lived in a three-room shack beside the river... ." The writer went on to reveal—openly and honestly—his story of a childhood of deprivation, yet he told it without animosity, only compassion for his parents who struggled daily for survival. "And I always had books to pull me through any perceived difficulties," he said. Ultimately, books became his life.

At George's invitation, Dick and I travelled down to his used bookstore, *Fair's Fair*, in Inglewood. We were gobsmacked at the magnitude of the operation—twelve-foot-high shelves covering 9,700 square feet, with five million books coming through the doors every year. It's a family affair with wife, sons, daughter, nieces, grandsons, and in-laws cataloguing and shelving the backbreaking volume. It brought me such warmth to know that the little kid from Lowery Gardens was living his dream. As we parted, I expressed my delight at witnessing his joy over owning his own bookstore. "Oh, I don't own the store," he said, chuckling. "It owns me."

Then one evening George called from his bed in Rosedale Hospice to tell me he was dying. He wanted to make one last connection with his friend. I was honoured. I miss my friend.

You'll remember the Dudder family, our next-door neighbours back in Connaught. They were another family struggling to make ends meet. You always spoke admirably of the parents working multiple jobs to feed their five children. Donnie, the eldest, and our Donnie were best friends and fellow adventurers as young boys. Brother Don forever applauded you and Mrs. Dudder for allowing your sons the freedom to explore, and just be boys.

I was preschool age during our Connaught years, so my memories of life there crop up only occasionally, in vignettes that are always cloudy. I couldn't put a face to Jimmy Dudder, but I remember him leading me across the street to his grandmother's place in the *President Apartments*. Having a grandma at all was pretty significant in my eyes, but when his grandma pulled a gigantic jar filled with jelly beans from her pantry and held it out to me, I thought I'd arrived in heaven. I can still feel the stickiness on my fingers as I pulled my chubby hands out of that jar.

Well, Mother, one day a few years ago, I came home to a voice on my answering machine: "Hello, this is Jim Dudder calling from Daysland." *Jimmy of the jelly beans*, I gasped! I had not seen or heard of Jimmy for over sixty years, not since we were five-year-old tikes together at Grandma's place. I called back and we set a date to meet.

Jim arrived at my home bearing copies of my book that he'd previously purchased for family members—he was keen to have them autographed. Getting to know Jim the adult, kind-hearted and warm, over tea and cookies in the sunroom, was an afternoon I'll never forget. He brought me up to date on all the members of this beautiful family. Far too soon after this meeting, my heart sank when I spotted Jim's obituary in the paper. "Rest in Peace, dear Jim," I whispered through tears. "I hope heaven is raining jelly beans."

This next story is probably one for Dad, but since I'm on the topic of readers, I'll tell it to you. Marg and Brian, a delightful couple living in the southwest community of Kelvin Grove, called me one day with an invitation to come for tea. When I arrived at their cozy home, they couldn't wait to lead me into their dining room, where they gestured toward their antique table laden with mementoes from Wainwright, Marg's hometown. You wouldn't believe the bounty: photos of the town, mementoes of Grandpa King's *Wainwright Dramatic Club*, handwritten letters from Aunt Millie, newspaper clippings of the King family, even copies of Dad's and Aunt Millie's obituaries. But they saved the best for last when they pointed to their wedding photo on display in the middle of the table, Marg drawing my attention to the beautiful lace trim on her gown. "That lace was very special," she said, "because your grandfather brought it all the way from England just to adorn my gown." Just when I thought I knew Grandpa King, I got to know him a little better—jewellery, antiques, trench art, and now lace! Nothing was outside his realm, was it? But the pièce de résistance was still to come: from the table, Marg lifted a small package wrapped in crinkly tissue, delicately peeled back the edges, and presented me with saved remnants of that very lace. I just got to know Marg a little better, too.

Finally, you'll be touched to know how *The House With The Light On* helped to fill the oppressive end-of-life days for two friends. Do you remember Don's friend Patsy from high school? The girl he fussed over for a week, designing her corsage for a sorority formal? The girl that married a mutual friend, and Don said it would never last? And it didn't? But by that time, Don had lost touch with them both. Patsy went on to marry a second time, and had two sons. But life was not kind to Patsy; she buried both her sons, and then her husband. Then in her twilight years, she stepped back into the life of her first husband—Don's friend—now gravely ill, and confined to a nursing home in Vancouver.

One day, while visiting him, she spotted a book at his bedside—*The House With The Light On*—sent to him from a cousin in Toronto. Since his eyesight was failing, she made reading to him the focus of her visits. Words from the book brought memories flooding back for both of them. After he died, Patsy resolved to reconnect with her old friend Don. The last word she had on his whereabouts was that he lived in Los Angeles. She tracked down a LA phonebook in the Vancouver library, but rolled her eyes when saw the mile-long list of Donald Kings. Still, she was undeterred, resolving to call them all—"Is this the Don King that lived in Calgary,

Canada, in the '50s?" On the third call, a familiar voice said yes! An old friendship was reborn.

I met Trudy in the summer of '58, when we were both student nurses affiliating at the Provincial Mental Hospital in Ponoka. As you know, I married the local boy that I met that summer. Well, so did Trudy. Art and Trudy settled into married life in Ponoka, Dick and I in Calgary. Throughout the busy child-raising years, contact with one another became sporadic. Then one black day, Art phoned to say that Trudy was suffering terminal cancer. I wrote to her the next morning, and sent her a copy of *The House With The Light On*. Art responded with gratitude, and the news that the family was reading it to her. When Trudy died, we traveled to Ponoka to attend her celebration service, following which we gathered with friends at the family home. As I walked in the door, Art, gripping my book, raised his hand to wave me in. Then his daughter, witnessing the scene, came rushing over. "Have you read this book?" she gushed, all out of breath. "It was written by a friend of my mother's. She sent it to us, and Dad and my brother and I would each read to her when we came to visit. We'd bookmark where we left off, and the next person would pick up from there." Then tearfully, she turned toward her dad and said, "This book was the one thing that brought a smile to Mom's face on her worst days, wasn't it, Dad?" He nodded in agreement. Then, wiping the tears from her cheeks, her face brightened as she turned back to me: "I'm sure you'd love this book, too," she said, "I'd lend you our copy, but we don't want it to leave our house." I thanked her for her consideration, and, patting her hand, said, "You know, I already have a copy. And you're right, I love it, too."

Just one more story, Mother. This one's a complete departure from the others, but I'm excited to tell you about it nevertheless. I know you always held fond memories of dear

Marion, your much-loved friend who lived with us for a few years when I was a young child. You used to say she called me "the peaceful little girl with the russet hair." (I'd like to think that I've lived up to her portrayal, although my hair's no longer russet.) As you know, Marion married and moved to a farm in Balzac where she and George built a little four-room brick house, which stood directly across the highway from the home of George's parents. Both hardworking families were dedicated to conscientiously working the land.

You'll remember the summer Marion and George invited Don and me to come and spend a week on the farm when we were kids, utopia for us pair of city slickers. We talked about our farm adventure forever after—sitting up on the big tractor, milking the cows, collecting the eggs, and trying to outrun the nasty rooster bent on pecking the back of my legs. A highlight was visiting the neighbouring farm where the woman of the house had a donut-making machine. I still salivate at that memory. One thing that especially intrigued me was Marion and George's raised front entrance to their house, where there were no steps leading up to the door. If you opened it from the inside and took a step, you'd plunge six feet into the stubble below. We understood, of course, that they never intended to use this door, so they kept it permanently bolted and that was that. Still, I always thought it looked a bit odd.

One day when Dick and I were travelling the highway, and passing the setting of the familiar farmhouses, our heads swivelled in bewilderment. Both houses were gone! Another chapter, we nodded. On subsequent trips, we witnessed large graders preparing the land for development. Then one day, I opened the morning newspaper to a full-page ad announcing: "*Cooper's Crossing*, where buyers are finding their dream homes at the most prestigious addresses in Airdrie." Don was now living back in Calgary, so I called him. "Guess where we're going today?" I said. "*Cooper's Crossing* in Airdrie!" "Cooper's what? Airdrie? I haven't been to Airdrie since I was a kid!" "You're right," I said, "so it's time. Get ready, I'm on my way." And so, Don and I made our second visit to Airdrie together.

We found an inviting new community, featuring a network of beautiful parkways weaving among its character homes. We were dazzled. Then we reminisced about our week on Marion and George Cooper's farm when we were kids. We wondered if they were looking down in awe at the transformation taking place on their land. Were they thunderstruck by this sought-after development honouring its history with their name? Were they, like us, missing their little brick house ... with no front steps?

Well, Mother, I've covered the waterfront, haven't I? There's always more, but there's always next time. I'll close with a couple of lines sent from readers that affirm the overriding theme of so many readers—a love of Calgary during its calmer, gentler days. Barbara said, "Everyone who reads your book will wish, as I do, that life in the '40s and '50s could return to console us all." Meanwhile, I sensed that Joan felt that life in the '40s and '50s *had* returned to console us all, at least fleetingly, when she said, "Thanks for making a lot of people happy with this book." I know the foundation of my story stemmed from my happy childhood, so it's really you and Dad they should be thanking. I'll do it for all of us—thank you, thank you!

Blessings, hugs, and all my love,
Eleanor

—Chapter Five—
Brother Don

Donald Emerson King

Born April 4, 1934—Calgary, Alberta, Canada
Died November 10, 2016—Calgary, Alberta, Canada

Dear Don,
 I was at the breakfast table when the phone rang at 8:30 a.m. You know better than anyone that a typical day for

your nocturnal sister rarely gets underway at this hour. But I'd scarcely slept, because Dick and I were bracing for a full day. It was moving day. We'd been five months in a rented condo, our refuge while our house was under restoration from that ruinous fire. Who could be calling? My friends never called at this hour—they knew better. I answered with a groggy, "Hello."

"This is the Calgary Police Service," a faint, gentle male voice greeted me. My heart raced as my mind sought possibilities that might prompt a call from the police. But the officer quickly moved the conversation forward. "Are you Mrs. Byers?" he asked.

"Yes, I am."

"Is Donald King your brother?"

"Yes, he is," I replied, beginning to hyperventilate.

"I'm sorry to inform you that Mr. King was found dead in his apartment this morning."

OMG! This isn't how I thought the end would come. I reached for Dick's comforting embrace.

You'd been hospitalized twice recently for aspiration pneumonia, a common complication of advanced Parkinson's Disease, when swallowing becomes difficult. I have to say you did not look well when Dick and I delivered you home last night. You and I spoke again later by phone, as you were preparing for bed—you were expressing concerns about managing a new strategy to prevent further pneumonia. I had said, "Don't worry, get a good night's sleep, and I'll help you with it when we talk in the morning." But morning didn't come for us. You slipped away in the night. I immediately thought back to your last doctor visit when you had turned to me in the waiting room and said, "You know, El, all I want to do now is sleep." It was a telling statement, a warning to me that your time was getting close. Now it was up—you were getting the sleep that you wanted.

Your advanced Parkinson's had brought you back home to Calgary, which had given us two good years together, after being separated by the miles, essentially our whole adult lives. We were better than most siblings at writing one another through the years, wouldn't you say? In fact, we were pretty darn good. Still, I'm now realizing there were gaping holes that the letters didn't fill. But before I try to fill them, I'm tempted to back up to the beginning, when we were living under the same roof.

You were born on April 4, 1934, three days after Easter Sunday, an easy date to remember: 04, 04, 34. I don't need to remind you that big brother Stan—age four and a half—was not an eager member of the welcome party. A baby brother was a poor excuse for what he'd previously ordered—either a polar bear or a porcupine. Dad did his best to appease him by saying, "But look! You got a red-faced lobster!" A bit of an ominous start, wasn't it? My coming along three and a half years later probably didn't help—I made you the dreaded middle child. Sorry.

I was pathologically shy as a kid, so from the beginning, I admired—and envied—your outgoing confidence. I stood head bowed and mute in the company of adults, while you were striking up a conversation about whatever was on your mind, with anyone willing to listen. When I recently reminded you of this glaring dissimilarity in our childhood personalities, I was shocked at your reply: "Oh, but I was intensely uncomfortable with kids my own age," you said. "Mother had to walk me to school twice a day for the first two weeks in Grade 1 at Connaught School, because I was refusing to go. I screamed all the way there. I was totally unnerved by all those kids around me."

You only survived that first year at Connaught through Mother's volunteer position as the Home and School's delegate to the League of Nations, which called for her to attend meetings at the school. "I loved meeting days," you said, "when I knew Mother was in the school. At 3:30 when school got out, I'd fly upstairs to the assembly hall on the top floor, push open the swinging doors, and scan the attendees until I spotted her. Then I'd squeeze in beside her for the rest of the meeting. The world of adults was such a relief, after a day with a bunch of kids. Finally, her meeting would break for refreshments, and I'd get to have cookies while Mother had tea. Afterward, we'd walk home together." That story confirmed what I always perceived—that Mother was your most understanding ally. Dad, on the other hand, never quite grasped what made you tick. I laughed when you told me about a childhood birthday party, although there is a sad element to it.

Your neighbour friend, King Woodside, invited you to his birthday party, which his grandmother, Mrs. Christie, was hosting in her fabulous home. Mother delivered you to the party, dressed in your best with gift in hand, assuming you'd be excited and happy to be included on the guest list. She didn't expect that you'd be even more uncomfortable in this setting than you were in your Grade 1 classroom. But, in fact, close quarters with this houseful of noisy kids became so intolerable that you snuck out the back door, and headed south up the alley for parts unknown. You were careful not to go home, fearing Mother would take you back to the party. What you hadn't counted on was a neighbour coming by in her car, spotting you, and, assuming you were lost, delivering you home. But you were a canny kid—you went in the back gate and faked opening the back door, pausing with your hand on the knob until she drove away. Then you were off again, this time securing a hiding spot where no one would find you. Then you waited. When you spotted some of the kids who'd been at the party, you knew it was safe to go home. "But surely Mrs. Christie would have discovered you missing," I said, poking holes in your story. "Didn't she call Mother?" "Oh, yes," you said, "she phoned Mother right away, terribly concerned, and apologizing profusely that I'd gotten away on her watch. But Mother surmised exactly what was going on, and calmly waited. I showed up eventually, like she knew I would. When I walked in the door, she said, 'Mrs. Christie called. She's feeling bad that you missed out on the cake and ice cream.'"

You liked to remind me of the freedoms you enjoyed, even during your preschool years when you meandered the neighbourhood like you owned it, stopping for sandwiches and conversation with a circle of women, who opened their doors to your charm. "I went somewhere down the street every morning for my mid-morning peanut butter sandwich," you told me, although you were no longer clear just who graced you with your favourite treat. "I didn't always give a full accounting of all the places I'd been," you said, "and Mother didn't show concern. It was a lovely freedom for a five-year-old." Then you'd wax on about how tragic it is that my grandchildren have been denied such liberties. We both agreed that our mother was vigilant, but she also trusted her instincts, especially when it came to your early idiosyncrasies. And it was the '30s, after all, when trust and safety were taken for granted in suburban Calgary.

You had one other favourite in your world of adults, but you didn't call on her, she called on you. You forever referred to her as *Mrs. Powell of the Dancing Dog*. For an impressionable five-year-old, Mrs. Powell—and her phantom concerts—triggered your first stirrings of interest in the world of entertainment. You described Mrs. Powell as a vivacious little woman who lived in reduced circumstances a couple of blocks north of us near the railroad tracks. When she got low on funds, she would make *tickets* by hand for a concert she was producing, and go about the neighbourhood selling them. "She would always come to our door, and Mother would buy two tickets," you said. "They were twenty-five cents each. Mother would invite her in, and her little dog would dance for us in the front hall. I was so enthralled with her dancing dog show that I begged Mother to take me to her concert, which I assumed would be spectacular." But there was an unusual twist to your happy story. When concert day arrived, Mother would quietly and patiently try to explain that she didn't think it was likely to take place. And sure enough, the concerts never materialized. "I was always a little confused," you said, "because Mother was reluctant to fully spell it out. But in time, I came to understand that it was Mrs. Powell's way of begging with dignity." Three years after your last encounter with *Mrs. Powell of the Dancing Dog*—and her concerts that never were—you made your own formal acting debut. It was Grade 3, Connaught School, a Christmas play called *A Substitute for Santa*. You were an elf.

We moved to Scarboro the summer before you started Grade 4, which meant a change of school from Connaught to Sunalta School. For a kid uncomfortable with kids your own age to start with, adjusting to a whole new circle must have been overwhelming. Miss Allison, the Grades Three and Four teacher, had taught those grades in the same room since Sunalta School opened in 1912. At least that's what we surmised. Her schedule never altered, as we read to her from the same readers and she read to us the same stories year after year. And we coloured the same pictures, being careful to stay in the lines. I know all this because I followed you into her classroom.

I assume Miss Allison, bless her, was equipped to teach the rudiments of reading and printing, but she was ill-equipped to make concessions for an atypical, unhappy child like you. And so, you floundered. At the end of the term, you were coldly handed a report card that read, "Failed." I can't imagine ever doing that to a kid. It's the teacher who's failed, not the child. You cried all the way home, of course. Mother, a former teacher, was shocked and devastated. Dad, a take-charge kind of guy, reacted the only way he knew how, by taking charge. Fully aware that you were anything but slow, he picked up the phone, and made an appointment with the school principal. The upshot of that meeting was a compromise, which you will remember—you were allowed to advance to Grade 5 under Miss Robertson, where you'd be rigorously monitored until Christmas, at which time you'd either continue on, or return to Grade 4. You immediately sensed that Miss Robertson was in your corner, and, with that assurance, you sailed through to Grade 6. Still, it wasn't all roses, was it? I think it would be safe to say that you hated school from a shaky beginning to an inglorious ending.

School would have been a breeze if you could have lived on English, social studies, and music, and dispensed with the maths and sciences. The system didn't accommodate a one-sided guy, did it? I still can't believe our high school principal's solution for you, after you essentially flunked most of Grade 10. He summoned Dad to his office, and said, "Mr. King, I think your son should drop out of school, and apply for work at a bank—he could establish a very satisfying career with a bank." Even today, I scarcely know how to comment. Anyway, Dad wasn't having any of it, and once again he went to bat for you. He put pressure on the school—and on you—to somehow make it to the finish line. But it was a struggle, wasn't it?

How many subjects did you repeat? More than once? Years after the fact, when a master's degree in fine arts had restored your self-esteem, you joked about your adventures in high school physics. Your teacher, J. Winston Churchill, demanded a perfect set of notes, which he examined with a fine-tooth comb at select intervals, stamping each page that met with his approval, "Accepted JWC." He assigned the identical set of notes year after year, so you borrowed your friend Mike's because he'd completed the course the year before. You copied every page of Mike's notes word for word, which JWC stamped, and in June, you wrote the final exam ... without Mike. You received a grade of 36 percent. You studied all summer, and the end of August, you wrote the supplementary exam, and got 35 percent. Your perfect set of *Accepted JWC* notes was worth nada. Well, you decided, there's more than one way to skin a cat. To cobble together enough credits for university entrance, you signed up for a correspondence cooking course. Remember that?

The one practical assignment was baking powder biscuits, which Mother emphatically insisted you fulfill without her assistance. But that didn't stop her from pacing the kitchen and looking over your shoulder, or me from heckling from the sidelines. You worked the dough to death, attacked it with a rolling pin, cut perfect circles, and into the oven they went. You watched the oven like a hawk, making sure you pulled them out when they were a perfect golden brown. Trouble is, they were hard as hockey pucks. But they looked good, so you packaged them up, and shipped them off to the Department of Education in Edmonton. I have to assume the person who taste-tested your works of art didn't want to risk breaking his or her teeth on a supplementary batch, so you were given a passing grade. We received our high school diplomas in the mail on the same day. Unfortunately, your diploma still did not meet entrance requirements for a Canadian university, so you sought a stepping stone to attain this goal. You found it in Spokane, Washington. Gonzaga was a private, modest-sized Roman Catholic university in a pleasant residential setting.

It was your first venture away from home. You held the distinction of being the only *Protestant Canadian* on campus, and in your Hudson's Bay blanket coat, stood out as the *Canuck in the red coat*. You were also the Canuck who was homesick. You and I hadn't always displayed the best examples of civility at home, but now we missed each other terribly. We began writing to one another regularly, a habit that we maintained forever after, and one that we both subsequently extended to our respective friends.

At Gonzaga you were finally able to enrol in a slate of courses that suited your interests, although after years of poor study habits, stemming from rebellion to courses outside your interest, it was a struggle. But you prevailed, finally scraping together enough credits to enter the Arts program at the University of British Columbia. You were finally on your way.

I'll never forget the summer of '56 when you filled your days packing for UBC. Where did Dad find that old trunk anyway? Was it hidden in the basement? My memory is of a well-worn, upright beast—black, with brass gaskets and leather pulls. You were in ecstasies over that trunk. I can still hear you thumping it up the stairs to your bedroom, standing it upright, and spreading it open. One side featured a compartment with beautiful wooden hangers, designed for jackets, pants, and dress shirts, and below that a drawer for shoes. The opposing side was filled with drawers for everything else. It stood gaping in your bedroom for weeks, as you selected your campus wardrobe. "These poky drawers don't hold half my sweaters," I could hear you muttering as you agonized over what you'd have to leave behind. Meanwhile, Mother and Dad agonized over whether you intended to study, or just look good. I have no idea how that trunk travelled out to Vancouver, or how you got it into you assigned room where you boarded. I wish I'd been there to see the expression on your landlady's face when you arrived with it. But you were ever the charmer with the ladies, and I know you won Mrs. Hankey over the first day regardless. In fact, you became forever friends. I never saw that trunk again. What happened to it?

Life changes were taking place for both of us during this period. You were adjusting to Vancouver's rain and UBC's intimidating campus, while I was adapting to slave labour six days a week as a student nurse at the Calgary General Hospital School of Nursing. We both had new adoptive mothers. You lived in the home of a lovely Australian couple and their lone teenaged son, where you were promptly embraced as a second son and big brother. I was confined to barracks with 250 sisters, under the watchful eye of a house mother, who laid down impossible rules and had eyes in the back of her head. You—who'd always been the pickiest eater on earth—had to fork your way through dishes you'd never before encountered. I could see you gagging the day you wrote to me about your last evening's menu of beef brains and toast. Meanwhile, I was wolfing down institutional food with abandon—taste was irrelevant in my perpetual state of hunger.

For the first time, I was really beginning to feel isolated from you. We still corresponded, but we both lacked the time and energy to write as often we had in the past. A sense of loss crept into the familiar pattern we had so comfortably shared. It was during these years that Mother and Dad faced significant changes in their own lives, both being stricken with major chronic illnesses: Dad was diagnosed with Parkinson's Disease and Mother was battling a mood disorder that was defying treatment. Stan was ensconced with Moral Re-Armament at Mackinac Island, Michigan, quietly and uncomplainingly sorting out his own life. All five of us were at pivotal stages in our lives, with no one other to lean on. Still, I knew that your adoptive family was caring for you, beef brains and all, and I had a permanent pack of *sisters* at elbows length, embracing me with love and laughter, regardless of the day's drudgery. The kids were okay.

You dribbled raindrops on your first letters to me from Vancouver, displaying your displeasure with the rain. You added an umbrella to your wardrobe. Eventually you got past

My visit to UBC

the wet, and grew to love your UBC experience. And you took the direct route to earning a Bachelor of Arts degree in English and Psychology. Your final summer on the West Coast delivered a dream job working with *Theatre Under The Stars* (TUTS) at the invitation of Hugh Pickett, your fraternity brother. This first exciting taste in stage management whetted your appetite for more, which you assumed meant further education. And so, you headed off to the East Coast and the graduate program at *Boston University's School of Fine and Applied Arts*. You didn't ship that big trunk all the way to Boston, did you? Just wondering.

When I think of your Boston years today, I am saddened with the uncomfortable fact that Mother and Dad were never really supportive of the path you were choosing for your life. I suspect their attitude was not uncommon at the time, and may prevail even yet. "The stage? But when do you plan to get a *real* job?" And the question that dogged you long into adulthood—the one you refused to dignify with a reply—"When are you going to find a nice girl and settle down?" You can thank me for diverting some of this unwanted attention from you when I found a nice boy and settled down. When I had a baby a year later, you entered *uncledom*, as you called it, with all the drama I'd come to expect from you. Our firstborn's arrival was the one and only occasion that you sprang for a long-distance phone call, a rare luxury in our worlds. Remember calling from your summer job at the Falmouth Playhouse on Cape Cod to the hospital where I was confined? You assumed a phone would be available at my bedside, or at the very least, the staff would deliver one there. Dreamer, you watched too many movies. Did I ever tell you the torture of walking that mile-long corridor to the nurse's station with a bottom full of stitches? Well,

I'm telling you now. But it was worth it. We laughed and cried together.

So as I was settling into domesticity, you were spreading your wings. Registration day at Boston U was quite an opener. Let's do it again: It was a stormy day such as you'd never experienced before, with a wind so severe you were picking your way along the sidewalk, clinging to lampposts, mailboxes, anything fixed to the ground, to keep you from blowing away. Sidewalks and roads were all but abandoned, and many stores had closed shop. You spotted a coffee shop with lights on, so you stumbled inside to take refuge. The coffee shop was empty, save for one idle waitress standing at the back, puffing on a cigarette. Gasping for breath, you explained to her that you were attempting to get to Boston U's registration office. "Well," she said, "not to worry—registration has been cancelled due to weather conditions anyway. You'll have to try again tomorrow." With a sigh of relief, you sat down and ordered a coffee and a donut. When the waitress arrived with your order, she said, "I'm planning to register tomorrow myself. Why don't we meet and go together?"

Touched with this total stranger's offer of moral support on such an unnerving start, you accepted. You met the next day and successfully registered together. It was then that you discovered that she, too, was enrolling in the fine arts program. And so, your paths crossed again in classes and workshops over the next two years. Eventually, you shared centre stage in Arthur Miller's

The Crucible. You wrote to me about the cast's collective case of the jitters on opening night. Arthur Miller was in the audience! The waitress cum actress was Faye Dunaway.

In Boston, you were finally enrolled in courses of interest with no physics or math to put the kibosh on a good thing. You were also surrounded by people who shared your enthusiasm for the theatre. I have found a stack of preserved playbills amongst your effects, attesting to the many acting roles and stage management assignments you were involved with—*Oedipus Rex, The Skin of Our Teeth, Happy as Larry, Henry IV...* . For your graduate thesis performance, you played the role of *Charles, the Dauphin*, in the North American premiere of the Christopher Fry translation of *The Lark,* by Jean Anouilh. You pulled off a glowing review. Today, when I see your name in print on all these playbills, I'm struck with the reality that I was scarcely aware of your world at the time. I was fully embedded in my own world—life as full-time wife and mother, focussed on making ends meet and maintaining a functioning home for my family. If only I could have hopped a plane to come see you as Charles, and brag, to Arthur Miller seated beside me in the front row, "That's my brother!" If only.

You graduated with a master's degree in fine arts in June 1962, with no fanfare, quietly celebrating your achievement without a single member of your family attending your commencement exercises. We should have been there. What were your thoughts on that day? That your family should have been there, or that we didn't belong there? Sometimes I wonder if you had preferred keeping that world to yourself. I wish we had at least talked about it. My one comfort now is recognizing how many wonderful friendships you established at Boston U, friendships you maintained for the rest of your life.

You had worked your way through Boston U as a room service waiter at the nearby *Braemore Hotel*. After graduation, your manager set you up with an interview at a sister hotel in New York City, *The Plaza*, which was seeking a page to assist the maître d' in the *Persian Room* nightclub. You landed the job, found a room at the YMCA to fit your budget, and reported for duty. It was September 1962. It had all happened so fast—New York City—city of lights, city of your dreams.

Your letters from New York were filled with tales of the latest stars playing the *Persian Room*, and the rich and famous seated ringside. You were dazzled by the celebrities on both sides of the velvet rope. I haven't forgotten your description of nineteen-year-old Liza Minelli gasping for air, her body in uncontrolled locomotion leading up to show time, then her abrupt transformation as she strutted on stage like a pro, belting out *Liza With a Zee*. Or her mother, Judy Garland, in outlandish garb, coming to see her daughter's show, accompanied by a circle of androgynous hangers-on half her age. But my favourite story was one you told of Rose Kennedy, mother of the then sitting president.

Mrs. Kennedy stopped by the nightclub late one evening, just wanting a plate of scrambled eggs. Mr. John, your temperamental boss, was never pleased when a customer did not plan to eat high on the hog, and take in the floor show as well. But this was Rose Kennedy, after all, so he offered a gracious welcome. You weren't prepared for what was about to take place after the eggs. As Mr. John assisted Mrs. Kennedy with her coat, she casually mentioned that she was looking forward to the walk back to her apartment. Mr. John, aware that she would not have a family member—or any security—to accompany her, wouldn't hear of her walking the streets of New York alone. "But Mr. John, it's only a seven-minute walk," argued Mrs. Kennedy, "and it's such a lovely, warm evening." "Then my boy Donald will accompany you," he said, whirling in your direction, and dismissing any further debate. You remembered it as the longest seven minutes of your life—Rose Kennedy marching boldly through the streets with you quivering at her side. I think of it as the only time in your life when the fearless conversationalist was at a loss for words. It took Rose Kennedy to get you tongue tied.

In spite of the nightly excitement of the *Persian Room*, you knew it would not be a long-standing career for you. Mr. John knew it, too, and encouraged you to reach out. And so began a series of ventures from guest lecturing in the drama department of the University of Minnesota to managing on- and off-Broadway shows, whether musical revues or fashion shows. The New York years were your profitable years, when you shopped for our children at *Brooks Brothers*, *Bergdorf Goodman*, and *FAO Swartz*. It so happened that your years of riches coincided with our years of poverty, as our family grew, and we took on a mortgage. I don't think I've ever told you this, but the duty charges we used to pay to retrieve your extravagant Christmas gifts from the Customs Office, exceeded our entire Christmas budget. But we'd laugh, and agree that it was worth every dollar to see the rapture on our little Doug's face, as he rode Uncle Don's motorized Stutz Bearcat around the rumpus room like he was A. J. Foyt. Except our A. J. burned through every battery in the house by Boxing Day, and tears were shed when the Stutz ground to a halt. That's when his resourceful dad mounted a rechargeable twelve-volt car battery onto a trailer, hooked it on behind, and the Stutz sputtered back to life.

The Christmas when your New York fashion sense kicked in, you sent Diane, age four, a beautiful navy knitted dress with white piping, and its matching coat. The *Bergdorf Goodman's* sales clerk saw *rich uncle* written across your forehead, and said, "Sir, there's a lovely matching beret for this outfit, and, oh yes, white leotards would add the perfect touch." "Of course," you replied. "Toss them in." Did it ever occur to you that I didn't own a 5th Avenue wardrobe to accompany my daughter on outings? I wanted to tack a postscript onto my thank-you notes—"Ahem … I'm a size eight." Well, never mind, big brother Doug was a suitable escort in his *Brooks Brothers* navy blazer with burgundy piping, white dress shirt with Eton collar, grey wool shorts, navy wool knee socks, and striped tie. Straight out of a British boarding school. Too bad he'd outgrown the Stutz Bearcat by this time. And how do you top engraved sterling silver stud boxes from *Tiffany's* arriving for the birth of each of our children? You must have heaved a sigh when we stopped at three.

Unfortunately, the celebrity and the lights of New York weren't enough to compensate for the anxiety and stress assaulting your nervous system. And so, in 1970, you packed your bags and moved to the West Coast—Los Angeles—where you hoped the pace would take mercy on your nerves. Assuming you'd made up your mind, I refrained from saying anything to you, but I couldn't shake the feeling that you belonged in New York, in spite of your anxiety. I'd seen you set your sights on the Big Apple from the time you were a kid—live theatre was in your blood just as it was with our Grandpa King. I silently cheered when you turned around a couple of years later, and headed back to New York to take another crack at it.

Your first letter back confirmed my belief. You were enervated by visits to old haunts in Boston and Cape Cod, before settling into a pilot project for a TV special. It didn't materialize, but you soon landed an opportunity to stage manage a musical revue—*Music Music*—at City Centre, which was right up your alley. I rejoiced, until your next letter arrived, and I could sense the tension already rising. "Endless problems," you wrote. "Dan Dailey, the star (remember him?) has so aged. In a rehearsal dance routine, he injured his Achilles tendon—he's out. Gene Nelson (remember him?) is in to replace him. Ira Gershwin and Irving Berlin want to withdraw their songs. Script conferences during all meals, 4.5 hours sleep a night. Insanity or unemployment. Never in-between. Exhausted."

You survived the revue, and then life delivered a project quite foreign to anything you'd done before. You couldn't wait to write to me all about it: "Robert Stigwood, producer of *Jesus Christ Superstar* has decided to get on the bandwagon of a new vogue in New York—female impersonators. (Remember Dad telling us about the Dumbbells?) Stigwood has booked my old *Persian Room* to try it out for the summer. I feel I've come full circle, although I can't picture female impersonators in the staid *Persian Room*. A cast of eight doing sixteen women, means changes during the show. Costumes and wigs are easy, but makeup means painting a whole new face. I don't know how they do it." The tension was really rising with your next letter: "Getting my first female impersonator show ready—*Manhattan Follies*—nearly finished me. They aren't your standard NY actors. Oh no! Never worked so hard in my life. Between shows they go down to the cafeteria in full drag, and the cooks freak out when they pass through the kitchen. The Plaza may never recover. The real Carol Channing got on stage at the end of one show with our Channing impersonator—you couldn't tell which was which. Our Judy Garland is so perfect it's frightening. Fans can hardly get through it, especially when Judy sings *Over The Rainbow*. Last night—our dark night—the director and I took Robin, the boy who does Marlene

Dietrich, to Danbury, Connecticut, to see the real Dietrich on opening night. For her encores, we were able to get Robin down front, sitting in the aisle where he could study her gestures at close range."

I knew that you had the talent to enjoy a fulfilling life in New York's theatre world, but I didn't want to address the one component that was always threatening from the sidelines—your battle with anxiety. Deep down, I knew that anxiety was part of your makeup for as long as I could remember, but I kept hoping that it would all go away with time and exposure to the stage. But it didn't, and the day came when you knew that your nervous system could no longer tolerate the buzz of New York. You had to escape to survive. And so, you returned to LA, this time for good. You would try your hand at scriptwriting, which took place on the West Coast.

It was a radical change for you. Gone from your wardrobe were the high-end Fifth Avenue threads, replaced by unconventional, almost bohemian duds purchased in thrift shops. I laughed when you told me what a good eye you had for spotting the best item on the rack in any given thrift store, a boast that didn't surprise me. Still, it took me a while to get used to your transformation. It may have been gradual, but you'll have to agree, it was radical. Which has me thinking about the time Stephen and I met you at the airport one year, when you were coming home for Christmas.

Stephen was about five years old—an age when a year between Christmases is a long time—and he couldn't remember what his Uncle Don looked like. So I gave him a description: "He's not a lot taller than Mommy, is very thin, and has a beard and dark hair in a ponytail. And he'll be wearing round, wire-rimmed glasses." Then I pointed to the doors you would come through after dealing with Customs.

Stephen sat in silence, his eyes peeled on the doors. When they suddenly sprang open, he was gone like a shot. I gasped as he flew to the feet of the first person to appear—a six-foot, 200-pound, clean-shaven giant—no ponytail, no glasses. If only you could have witnessed what happened next! Stephen looked up … way up, studied this stranger who filled the doorway, and then, shaking his head with indignation, bellowed, "You're not my Uncle Don!" The guy was understandably puzzled, but regrettably, he was also humourless. Without so much as a word or a pat on the head, he sidestepped Stephen, and continued on his way. Stephen sulked back to his mother, who was gasping for air, in stitches.

I should have prepared the poor kid for a long wait, knowing that you were always the last to come through those doors. Remember? You were always in the clutches of a Customs Officer. They profiled you every time as some latent druggie from Woodstock, concealing cocaine in the lining of your bags. When nothing turned up there, they'd open all your beautifully wrapped Christmas gifts. Such an exercise you'd go through. You refused to change your look, but you learned to bring your gifts unwrapped.

I wish we could have seen more of each other during your LA years, but we did connect at Christmas, and you came for summer visits when you could, to our cottage or to the mountains. Dick's company was conveniently headquartered in LA, so he connected with you on his business trips, and I joined him when possible. For the kids, nothing topped the vacation to Disneyland—stage managed by Uncle Don—back in the '70s. The rides in your little Sunbeam convertible were almost as much fun as the rides in the park. Beyond those fleeting times together, we settled for sharing our day-to-day lives through letters. Even so, during your forty-plus years in California, I never felt that I was fully grasping your world. How were you actually filling your days? Who were your friends? But now as I re-read your mountain of letters, I'm comforted by the long path of pages we walked together. We were more in tune with one another than I realized.

At the forefront of your letters was the family. You followed everyone's celebrations and concerns, whether it was the aging senior generation, the new generation of nieces and nephews, or the *sandwich generation* caring for both. You never failed to respond fully to family news that I sent you, whether celebrating our joys, commiserating with our sorrows, or offering brotherly advice. A typical letter would begin, "Thanks for your letter of October 18. Sorry to hear that Stephen's Grade 1 teacher is striking fear into those poor little kids just starting out. Don't get me started on teachers. Or schools." And you always gave a personal response to letters the kids sent you: "Dear Doug, Diane, and Stephen: Thanks for your three great letters. I have bachelor friends who say that letters from their nieces and nephews are often dull, badly constructed and make no sense, so I'm quite proud that mine are so polished and erudite."

When Stephen wrote to tell you, as only he could, that he just got braces on his teeth: "Dear Stephen, Thanks for your great letter. I took the liberty of asking Marcia, my neighbour who writes comedy, for her opinion on which of your names she thought the funniest—Tinsel Teeth, Brace Face, Tin Grin, Metal Mouth or Railroad Tracks (chew chew). She thought all your names were a scream and really clever, but neither of us could make up our minds...."

When Smokey, the children's beloved eighteen-year-old cat died, they were consoled by your response: "A marvellous letter from Diane contained the news of Smokey's new adventure. What a great family he had for his first life; I can't imagine it being topped in the other eight!"

And then the children grew up. "Enjoyed a letter from Stephen in early October, beautifully written, his bone-dry wit peeking out at every turn. It was such a pleasure to be in on his thirtieth birthday. Although I found him quiet, as always, he'd taken on a new polish—his manners, perfect; his sense of protocol, unerring. And the handsome features had settled; the little-boy was gone. Our Prince Valiant has indeed come of age."

Your sense of humour cropped up regularly: "Thanks for the pic of you and me in front of a pink cow in Calgary. How could we not look good?" "I called Mother to wish her a Happy Birthday. We talked about the New Year's Eve party she and I went to at Bethany Care Centre (where she was living) a couple of years ago, when I danced with the nurses. I told Mother they thought I was one of the residents. Mother said she didn't know how they could make that mistake. Anyone who lived at Bethany, and could dance that well, would dance out the door!" Wasn't it good that Mother could make light of her own situation now and then?

Death. It's difficult for everyone, but I think it was especially so for you. Would you agree? On returning to LA after Dad died, you wrote: "I'm trying to make sense of the week in Calgary. It isn't easy because I don't know how I feel. Thanks to Dick, Doug, Diane, and Stephen for getting you and Stan and me through that difficult week. Aren't they a splendid foursome!" Less than a year later, Mother was approaching her final days, and you wrote, "An old friend called from New York to see how I was doing. When I observed that I was not doing so well the second time around, he said, "One never does; it isn't until you've lost both parents that you become a grownup. Until then, you're always someone's child."

You also had a habit of scanning the newspapers for articles of interest over your routine morning coffee at the deli up the street, which you'd clip and save to enclose in your next letter. The deli's other patrons must have read a paper full of holes. The articles were always pertinent to my world—child-rearing, the pros and cons of home-schooling, the care of elderly parents. When I took up writing in the '80s, you began stuffing envelopes with material written either by, or about, authors. Soon we were exchanging ideas for possible projects. We celebrated one another's writing successes, and we both knew the sting of rejection. It, too, kept us connected. By the time you were into script writing, my children were in their teens, and fancying themselves TV aficionados. They began sending you storyline ideas for new TV shows, which you examined thoroughly and acknowledged with gratitude. Now and then, you even pitched the odd idea of theirs to an appropriate producer. Alas, we never saw one make it all the way to the small screen.

Since drama was in your blood, you were drawn to the pomp and ceremony of the Royal Family, always a favourite topic of conversation in your letters. Of course, drama was only half of it—we were products of our English heritage. The Royals were in our blood. The most prominent photos in our restaurant were those of Queen Victoria and Prince Albert, and remember the picture of King George VI and Queen Elizabeth with the princesses Elizabeth and Margaret that hung over Mother and Dad's bed? Whatever happened to that picture anyway? Amazing how some things just disappear. A Royal wedding, a coronation, or a funeral produced a minimum of two full pages from you.

You had no patience with US reporters who repeatedly got accounts of the Royals all wrong. You'd throw up your arms in despair, then extend a hand of charity saying, "Never mind, they simply don't get it. They haven't been steeped in royal protocol as we have." Of course you'd immediately throw up your arms again, adding, "But they should make it their business to learn more." Once in a while, when you couldn't stand a reporter's bumbling account, you'd write a letter to an editor to set him or her straight: "Your journalist has misreported the queen's arrangement for Diana's divorced parents at the wedding of Charles and Diana. In the interest of getting it right …" Then you'd proceed to get all the parties in question in their correct carriages, accompanied by the correct royal.

Occasionally, you included a history lesson with an accounting of the queen. One of your letters written in the '70s began, "Happy Dominion Day." I'd almost forgotten the forerunner to "Canada Day." The highlight of your letter was seeing "Her Majesty" on TV attending the Queen's Plate at Woodbine. "She may well be the last British sovereign to rule Canada," you wrote. "The French Canadians will eventually demand it to even the score from the Battle of the Plains of Abraham, and they will be right. I suppose we must come of age and let go our mother's hand. But for me it would be an awful rending. It's still an unmatched life of grace and discipline."

I hate to be the one to break the news, but on September 8, 2022, we had to let go her hand. Our beloved Queen Elizabeth II, age ninety-six, died at Balmoral Castle. And I don't need to tell you what an awful rending it was. You chose the very words most often repeated by the masses who queued for hours and days and miles to pay their respects where she lay in state at Westminster Hall—"a life of grace and discipline." She had buried her beloved Prince Philip, age ninety-nine, a year prior and celebrated her Platinum Jubilee in February. Then she began to visibly fail. But she had one final duty—to receive her new prime minister. She received Liz Truss—her fifteenth prime minister—on

Tuesday, allowed a day for her family to congregate, then on Thursday, closed her eyes. An unbelievable life ... and death.

I won't attempt to write an accounting of the pomp and ceremony to follow the queen's death—I'm beyond inadequate for such an assignment. But knowing your appetite for Royal occasions, plus your knowledge of Royal traditions and pageantry, I can see you already conjuring your own images of the affair. So I will give you just one word of advice—whatever you're conjuring in your mind's eye, increase it tenfold.

So we have a king again. We loved and admired George VI on the throne when we were kids. Now his grandson is the new monarch. Charles III is well prepared for the job. Even during his acute time of grief, he travelled throughout Britain carrying the goodness of his mother, greeting his subjects and pledging his dedication. He will be fine. God save the king.

One last memory, while we're on the Royals—do you remember the time I wrote to you after seeing the movie *Anne of the Thousand Days*, asking for clarification on Anne's daughter. On two long, yellow foolscap pages, you lay out the entire British Royal succession to the throne with a full accounting of each member. (All this before the advent of GOOGLE.) And across the bottom, you scratched, "Here endeth the lesson!" Not quite—you have to add Charles III.

Our mutual love of books and movies probably provided the most fodder for conversation. I'm bowled over by the number of books we read and movies we saw together, a thousand miles apart. Almost every letter travelling in either direction carried comments or recommendations for a great book "you've just got to read" or movie "you must see." Your critiques of movies were press-worthy, your trained eye catching every nuance. "Knocked me out, don't miss it," you'd say, or "Every frame takes your breath away." Other times, you'd name three movies you'd seen, noting, "You could miss all three and not feel you had lost out on life." When you saw your old friend Faye Dunaway in *The Eyes of Laura Mars*, you were horrified at the photography, costumes, makeup, everything. "She should sue," you said. I laughed at your comment on *The Last Temptation of Christ*: "What never works for me is New York accents with robes and sandals!"

Occasionally, you'd throw in a piece of nonsense for my entertainment: "Remember Lizabeth Scott, she of the sleek blonde hair and pouty lips (*Dead Reckoning* with Humphrey Bogart)? She was in front of me at the cash register at the local drugstore the other day. She still had the great hair, but the ravages of the plastic surgeons through the years had taken a terrible toll on the beautiful face."

It goes without saying that we were Academy Award junkies. You lived in Oscar land, and I lived in Calgary, but we attended the annual event together, competing for bragging rights with our respective predictions. If I say so myself, I gave you a pretty good run, considering I was the amateur. But I couldn't compete with your elaborate commentaries, like the one you gave to *Cabaret* in 1972: "For a musical I would call it quietly stupendous. Musicals on film have always embarrassed me somehow. I sink down in my seat during the songs. Singing in the rain is fine on stage, when believability has been suspended to begin with, but when transferred to the realism of film, it all becomes a bit silly. It can't stand up. But *Cabaret* works. The songs belong. They belong because they carefully remain within the framework of the cabaret, pointing up and heightening in perfect counterpoint, various aspects of the insidious, creeping paralysis of Naziism." Then you rambled on for another full page discussing the screenplay, the stars, the camera work, lighting, costumes, sets, makeup... ending with, "On Oscar night next April, it will be clean-up time for *Cabaret*." You were close. Liza Minelli won best actress, Joel Grey best supporting actor, and Bob Fosse best director, but Marlon Brando and *The Godfather* got in the way of a sweep.

I responded to that letter with a suggestion that you take a crack at becoming a film critic/analyst. You answered by return mail: "Writing a sister is stress free," you said, "but writing to deadline for *The Times* would be fraught with anxiety." There's that word again!

You especially revered the old stars of our youth, and mourned their passing. Oscar night, 1983, you wrote: "The tributes to Hepburn, Taylor, and Mastroianni were worth the price of admission." When Ingrid Bergman died: "The television last night was awash with her film clips. I want to sit forever in a darkened room watching endless reruns of *Casablanca* and command time to stand still." And after the death of Rita Hayworth: "Our Rita is gone. Will your kids ever have Ritas to remember?"

You regularly stepped away from the theatrical stage to comment on the world stage as viewed in your morning newspaper at the deli. You were especially keen to keep current with Canadian news, but it was a challenge because Canada frequently didn't rate as newsworthy in California. And when it did, you were never certain of its accuracy. Remember the lengthy article on Calgary that you sent me?

Some journalist wrote about this amazing city up north in Canada that had a network of underground tunnels connecting all of its downtown buildings. You couldn't believe that you didn't know about this feature of your hometown. The writer, if he had visited Calgary as he claimed, would have seen that our Plus 15s were above ground, not below. He based his entire story on a falsehood.

When Canada did make press in your newspaper, you not only let me know, but you had something to say about it. You spoke often of Pierre Trudeau, father of our current prime minister, perceived by Americans as "an impressive statesman with a global vision for Canada." You couldn't help wondering if this would be your view of him if you were living in Canada. Your last Trudeau comment came in a letter of November 1, 2000: "You know how often I complain that Canadian news doesn't make it to the outside world. Such was not the case with the death of Joseph Philippe Pierre Yves Elliott Trudeau—a full page in the *Los Angeles Times*." And when Peter Lougheed, our premier, made the front page of the *LA Times*, you were all over it. The article was entitled: "Oil-rich Albertans Wary of Poorer Canadian Cousins." You were surprised by the statement: "Only the Persian Gulf states of Kuwait, the United Arab Emirates, and Qatar have higher per capita incomes than Albertans."

Occasionally, you were shocked—and annoyed—when you learned of things about Canada that had been kept from us. "Following a news piece, 'The American government last week officially recognized their wrong treatment of Americans of Japanese descent after Pearl Harbour,' Stanley Meisler—*Los Angeles Times* foreign correspondent—was prompted to point out the parallel problem in Canada. Why didn't I know about that when I was growing up?" I'm prompted to point out that we also didn't learn anything about the treatment of our Indigenous people, did we? Shameful stories swept under the rug.

You reserved much of your political comment for the US, which you'd dramatize, sometimes irreverently, as when Jimmy Carter ran for office: "The presidential election is upon us. Of course, I'd prefer a Democrat in the White House, but not this time. I'll stick with Ford. A *born again* president is too terrifying even to speculate. Surely nothing could be more horrifying than a leader who thinks he has God on his side! Well, enough from old acid tongue." When you wrote about Ronald Reagan's inauguration, the television coverage—bouncing between that event and the freeing of the Iran hostages—impressed and captivated you: "Hours and hours without a hitch—either audio or video—or a slip from the anchor people who just kept talking, smoothly filling up the spaces of airtime. Endless cuts between the Reagans and the hostages—a hostage struggling down the steps of the plane, terror, happiness and confusion written all over his face, and in heart-stopping contrast, Nancy Reagan entering the inaugural ballroom serenely confident in her borrowed $10,000 Galanos gown and diamonds in her hair—television as it was meant to be at its apogee in the twentieth century." Whew! I betcha don't remember saying all that!

And every now and then, out of left field you'd insert a tidbit that would glaringly reveal your viewpoint on some issue you'd been mulling over. During the 1980 Olympics you wrote: "I'm watching the Winter Olympics (in Lake Placid, NY) when I can. The Read boy (Calgary's Ken Read) losing his ski was just awful … and Randy Gardner falling. I do wonder if it isn't a bit too much, striving for momentary perfection. It's such a joyous experience for us, the watchers, but the athletes seem almost beyond that, into a territory of the mind I'm not sure we understand ... and of course their lives so totally thrown off balance to get there." And after the 1996 Olympics, you wrote: "Little ninety-pound gymnast Kerry Strug's moment in the sun—perfect landing on one foot was pure theatre. The question is, was it also child abuse?"

You never made yourself the focus of your letters, but you also didn't hide your daily grind from me. Receiving your letters piecemeal over time, though, somehow screened the magnitude of your struggle. Now, reading them in one batch, your day-to-day grind comes home to me, as never before—the perpetual struggle to crack the impossible world of script-writing, never mind the battle for life's basics—food and rent. I'm thankful that you trusted me to be your sounding board. I knew you were at a low point the time you closed one letter saying: "You are not to be concerned, I don't need any money, I am picking up odd jobs and I'm fine." Sometimes you used a little King black humour in an attempt to soften your situation: "Hopefully I will do a couple of Industrials soon, either that or beg on the street." Between the lines, it wasn't funny.

Today, I see a forty-year chronicle of script submissions, new ideas, hopeful possibilities, endless waiting, then hopes dashed. Over and over ... and over again: "I'm up for assignment for a new Lear nightly soap." "The script went in a few days ago, so we'll see what develops." "I'm crossing my fingers." "I'm holding my breath." "Trying to sell yourself for 15 years is a bit of a drag." "I don't know where I am with my work anymore, except tired." "Appreciated your call of Sunday night to cheer me up. It got me through." You finally landed a script for the popular series *Maude*, but it was followed by a year of story conferences, endless outline changes, multiple rewrites. The good news is it brought you a nomination for a Humanitas Award. Bravo!

Thankfully, your stage-managing experiences landed you a live gig or two to keep the wolf from the door. Your Chevy Chase story should have been up for an Oscar: "I was pulled out of retirement by New York friends recently to stage manage the taping of a television show starring Chevy Chase—live audience in a Hollywood nightclub. Madness! With cameras rolling, Chevy is in the wings where I'm trying to attach an enema bag filled with green coloured water under his arm, beneath his shirt, with the attached tube leading down into his pants—beautiful white slacks. As he talks to the audience, he's to press his arm against the bag and wet his pants <u>green</u>! As they're calling a five-second warn on my headset, Chevy's screaming, 'the tube is leaking!' As I'm trying to stop the leak and shove him on stage, out of the corner of my eye, I see out the open stage door, a burly cop arresting a hooker across Sunset Strip; he's busily searching through her little gold lamé purse! Only in Hollywood!"

And speaking of Hollywood—the city that reviles aging—you fit in perfectly with your eternally youthful look. You also got away with it because you had no children to date you. Your lying caught up with you, though, when your *younger* sister's firstborn reached an age that placed her at age twelve when she had him. Your solution was simple—you made me your *older* sister. Thanks a lot. Forever after, you signed every birthday card to me, "… with love from your baby bro." But I had to give you legitimate strokes when you walked into a liquor store at age thirty-seven and the owner asked to see your ID. "The poor man must have been blind," you wrote, " but I'm making the most of the story." Then at age forty-seven, more flattering words: "A friend of mine, an actor of an age never discussed, who is a facelift buff, told me that the best time to have the eyes done, even if you don't appear to need it, is before you're forty. He strongly suggested that I take his advice 'when the time comes.' Do you suppose he's had his eyes done so often that it's affected his sight?" One week before your fiftieth birthday: "Dear El: A quick note to you while I have a few drops left of youth and sanity!"

Together in Hawaii

Ten years later, something came along that had a say about that endless youth that you enjoyed. It was called Parkinson's Disease. We had witnessed Dad's journey with Parkinson's, but I had blissfully dismissed any notion of a genetic factor. I have since learned that 15 percent of sufferers have a family history of the disease. Late in the day, I also learned that anxiety and Parkinson's often travel hand in hand. You and I remember Dad's disturbing anxiety attacks when we were teenagers, and how they were ultimately the precursor to the disease. Remember the summer we holidayed in Coeur d' Alene and poor Dad just paced the whole time? We could see his anguish, but didn't know how to help him. I remember him saying he felt like someone was stretching an elastic band inside his head, then letting it go with a snap. I can only imagine your terror when you began

We Three Kings: big brother Stan in cap.

experiencing similar symptoms, not your familiar everyday anxiety, but unprovoked, disabling attacks that sparked memories of Dad. And you were doing your level best to hide it from me.

As you know, you were the ultimate keeper of paper—medical records, dental records, tax files, manuscripts (half a dozen drafts), business letters, personal letters, and notes on everything under the sun. And of course, you left them all behind. You know me well enough to know that I would pick through every page of all nineteen boxes before disposing any of it. You're welcome. I will say this: you had everything organized and labelled, so as I'm sitting here wanting to chat with you about your Parkinson's journey, all I have to do is reach for your box labelled *Parkinson's*.

One folder in this box contains three headlines printed in thick black felt pen: *Like Father Like Son*, *Running in Deep Water*, and *Portrait of Parkinson's*. I see you were writing the story of your journey with the disease, and had not yet settled on a title. Your manuscript paints a clear picture, and I can't tell you how much it saddens me. You had developed an unfamiliar anxiety that was worrying, but when you developed a slowness in your walk, a sensation you described as "running in deep water," that cemented your own diagnosis of Parkinson's. You presented your concerns to both your primary care doctor and your psychiatrist, but both dismissed you, saying, "Your concern about Parkinson's is understandable, Mr. King, considering your father suffered from the disease. But I see no evidence to suggest that you have it." You knew otherwise. After two years of false assurances that you did not have the disease, you insisted on a referral to a neurologist.

You wrote about that first encounter on October 9, 1996, age sixty-two: "What seems to be the problem?" the neurologist asked. "My father had Parkinson's Disease," I said, "and now I have it." The neurologist, startled with a self-diagnosing patient, tempered the situation by labeling your slowness as "motor tension" or perhaps a form of "Parkinsonism." It's interesting to me that when Dad's history with the disease should have raised a red flag for your doctors, it instead did the opposite. They viewed you as a neurotic, imagining you had what your father had. Subsequent visits eventually revealed more pronounced bradykinesia (slow movement) followed by a new set of symptoms entering the picture—intermittent slight tremours of the left hand; micrographia (cramped handwriting); puckering feeling (tension) around the mouth; difficulty swallowing; slurred speech, especially when under stress; weight loss. My goodness, did it take all that to persuade your neurologist to take the next step? Finally, he prescribed Parkinson-specific medication to test the effects. Positive results quickly delivered a convincing diagnosis.

Throughout these years, I was witnessing changes in you during our brief and too infrequent visits together, either in Calgary or Los Angeles. I was recognizing the familiar Parkinson look that you were taking on, and more than once I asked if you'd been assessed for Parkinson's. Your quick reply was, "Yes, I have, and they say I don't have it." Looking back, your answer may have been truthful early on, but the long and short of it is, you wanted to keep the diagnosis from me. In fact, you did not share this information with anyone, not even your closest friends in Los Angeles. My eyes welled up when I found scribbled on one page of your Parkinson's notes: "My decision is to tell no one. I don't want to be defined by the disease." You chose a lonely path. It brought to mind another path that I watched you walk alone … your whole life.

From the time we were teenagers, I had assumed that you were gay, yet in spite of being best friends, we never talked about it. I never thought I should be the one to raise the subject, so I waited—leaving the door open for you. You never stepped through. Family members occasionally asked, "Why doesn't he 'come out' anyway?" One side of me wanted to ask the same question, then the other side would respond, "Why should he? Whose business?" Always I contented myself with the certainty that you knew, regardless whether you "came out" or "stayed in," that your sister loved you unreservedly. But when I read your Parkinson's note, "I don't want to be defined by the disease," a light went on, and I wept. You didn't want to be defined by your sexual orientation either. And we both know that you would be. I'm so sorry.

And so, returning to your Parkinson's Disease, you ventured forth on a long, lonely path with only one ally, a neurologist who initially dragged his feet. You recorded every visit with him—detailed accountings of physical examinations, blood pressure readings, and lengthy discussions of prescribed medications—dosages, scheduling, effects and side-effects. From day one, it was your mission to be a full participant in the management of your condition. You also pored over literature on Parkinson's, frequently arriving for your doctor visit armed with the latest information, likely clipped from your morning newspaper. I remember you doing the same thing for Dad long years ago. Thanks to your research on his behalf, he was an early recipient of both cryosurgery to arrest his hand tremors and the drug Sinemet to further ease symptoms of the disease. Now you were seeking the latest advances in treatment for yourself.

In spite of family members and friends witnessing your obvious—though unexplained—decline over an eighteen year period, you resisted sharing the truth with us. You deprived yourself of an embracing support system. Nothing is better managed in the dark. (OK, we've been through this before.) Then you began falling. You miraculously escaped broken bones, but eventually a serious fall delivered you to hospital, where you were placed in the care of a new circle of doctors. Recognizing the advanced state of your Parkinson's, they understood the pitfalls of discharging you back home. And so they began addressing the need to transfer you to a long-term care facility. Since I'd been agitating for years for you to move back home, you now acknowledged that home was the more inviting option. And so we set the wheels in motion.

From here in Calgary, I had a pretty accurate picture of the state of affairs fifteen-hundred miles away—your small bachelor pad packed to the hilt with life's essentials, a mile-high stash of manuscripts and books, and a lifetime of collectibles. Overwhelming to be sure. Lucky for both of us, three good men in our lives stepped up to the plate. I don't think I ever told you about Cousin Frank's idea: "I'll send down a truck," he said, "pack everything up, and deliver Don's belongings to a storage rental here. You can fly down and collect him, and once he's settled in, we'll deliver his things—a few boxes at a time—to sort through at his leisure. I'll arrange it all," he assured me. Isn't that our Frank? Just do it!

Unbeknown to us, however, Cousin Nick, your big-hearted ally in L A was already hauling bags and boxes—under your stage management—off to Goodwill, used bookstores, the dump, wherever ... effectively dismissing Frank's plan. You were clearly bent on culling *before* your move. That's when the third good man—actually my number one—came up with the a plan neither of us could refuse: "Let's hook up our fifth-wheel trailer," Dick said, "drive down to LA, load it up with Don's belongings, and then he can travel back with us in the trailer."

When I proposed this idea to you by phone, it was the first time in weeks that I could hear a sigh of relief in your voice. You loved this plan. And so I set a September date for our arrival. "Oh, but I can't be ready by then," you said. "We'll have to wait until spring." But I wasn't going to hear of you spending another winter alone, so I gave you an October deadline. "We'll have to pull out of LA by mid-October latest," I said, "or we'll risk running into winter conditions en route home." You agreed, reluctantly, and buckled down with Nick's help to the monumental task before you. Meanwhile, Dick and I were a comedy team preparing for the trip at our end in Calgary. Before setting forth on previous camping trips, we habitually stuffed our roomy rig with enough requisites for every possible eventuality. Now we were operating in the reverse—picking through our supplies for what we could leave behind. The mission was to leave optimum cargo space for you and your belongings. We pulled out of Calgary with the barest of essentials.

We moseyed down the US I-15, a route we'd travelled many times, stopping at favourite restaurants and campgrounds. I was a joyful, relaxed vacationer by day, but when I crawled into bed at night, I became anxious and sleepless, mulling over the logistics of the approaching move. I knew that we couldn't possibly haul a large trailer through the streets of Los Angeles, and certainly not up the long, narrow, steep driveway leading to your apartment tucked behind the property's boarding house. While I tossed all night, ruminating over potential problems, Dick was sleeping soundly because he only saw solutions. "I have a strategy all worked out," he said one night. "It's a bit complex, but it's feasible." I trusted him and finally got a night's sleep.

We pulled into a campground about an hour outside of Los Angeles—scenic and serene—where we'd stayed on previous occasions. Then Dick unhooked the trailer and set to work removing its large hitch bolted into the bed of the truck. This was no easy task, but necessary to free up invaluable space in the bed of the truck. All part of his plan. The following morning, we jumped into the truck, and set out for LA, leaving the trailer behind. I will never forget that day. Cousin Nick was out front to greet us, and direct Dick up to your narrow driveway to the cramped parking space near your stairwell. Only Dick could manoeuvre that truck through such close quarters unscathed. You appeared, looking pale and impossibly thin, wearing a baseball cap, an item you'd never worn in your life. Apparently a friend had plopped it on your head as a farewell gesture. It gave you such an unfamiliar, even bizarre, look, I almost wondered who you were. Then we set to work.

It was 32 C above, but felt like 40 when we stepped into your stifling apartment—to a ton of boxes, packed and stacked, in wait. I lost count of the number of times I trekked up and down that steep flight of concrete stairs to get them from your apartment to the truck. We filled the bed of the truck to overflowing, threw a tarp over top, and strapped it all down. Then we started filling the cab of the truck, wedging one thing or another around and under my space in the front seat, doing our best not to encroach on Dick's territory as the driver. We stuffed the entire back seat with soft goods—clothing, towels, blankets and such, which offered padding for your one precious commodity, a Tiffany lamp that you'd plucked from a garage sale. We saved just enough room for your 110-pound frame to crawl in, and flop onto the heap. We were ready to leave LA, but not before a farewell dinner with Nick.

You and Nick had enjoyed a wonderful friendship through the years, and as your health declined, Nick was there for you through thick and thin. His Christmas dinners were legendary—turkey with all the trimmings and pumpkin pie, served on his mother's china, with crystal and silverware gracing a table draped in red linens. Now the time had come for the two bachelor cousins to part company. Nick led us to a great little restaurant that offered a place to park our cumbersome cargo, and all four of us collapsed in exhaustion behind tall menus. While we clicked glasses, toasting good times past, and hopes for the future, I said a silent prayer that the truck wasn't being looted. It wasn't. Then we all gave Nick a grateful hug, you donned your out-of-character baseball cap, and we were off.

Poor Dick, I was so busy waving goodbye to Nick and the lights of LA that I neglected my job as navigator. Remember how we got royally lost, weaving our way down pitch-dark streets that kept leading to dead ends? I suggested maybe LA must not have been quite ready to let you go. Finally, we magically stumbled onto the freeway leading back to our campground. We rolled up to our campsite at some ungodly hour, the three of us numb with exhaustion. We pulled on our night attire, I heated up some hot chocolate, and … wouldn't you know it, the pull-out couch that was to serve as your bed, would not pull out. No amount of pleading was going to budge it. You waved us off to bed with a shrug, crawled onto the couch as it was, pulled up a blanket, and you were done. We booked an extra day in the campground to prepare for the long trek north. The first task of the morning was to transfer the heaping load in the truck bed to the trailer's storage spaces. I'll never forget Jim, a campsite neighbour, spotting Dick hard at work, and coming on the dead run to help. He didn't ask *if* he could help, or *how* he could help, he just dove in. Jim was Mexican, a retired firefighter, and he packed more boxes of every size and shape into the square footage of our trailer's storage area than it could possibly hold. He didn't leave a breath of wasted space. And he did it all with a giant smile on his face. We've hauled our trailer all over North America, from the southern US to Alaska, set up camp in countless campgrounds, and the one thing we have consistently experienced is the kindness of fellow campers. They travel with an unwritten code: "Help thy neighbour." Jim was the finest example of this, wasn't he? Dick's final task was to re-bolt the cumbersome hitch back into place in the truck bed, then ease the truck back to hook on the trailer. Click! That gave you and me time to sit at a picnic table to review your required documents for re-entering Canada, and prepare a list of your possessions for Customs. At day's end, Jim was back with his strapping son to muscle open the couch pull-out. He wanted you to start your journey with a good night's sleep.

Everything that hadn't made it into the trailer's outer storage, we'd hauled inside and packed into every nook and cranny. Remember how you and I crammed your entire hang-up wardrobe into our bedroom closet, which we'd left empty for you? And how a few miles down the road, the bar collapsed under the strain, and the whole works spilled out onto the floor? Without any fuss, Dick trotted off to a hardware store for a sturdier bar, and had the whole thing fixed before lunch. But that's his specialty—fixing stuff without a fuss.

When I think back on that trip, you really were a trooper. Leaving behind the country that has been home for over fifty-five years is a major upheaval for any eighty-year-old, but for a guy prone to anxiety and suffering from advanced Parkinson's Disease, the disruption could be catastrophic. Yet you found your own way of coping. As we pulled out of the campground, I could see that you were already closing the book on life in Los Angeles—you sat quietly, eyes forward, never looking back. You were readying for your final act in Calgary. It was even your first time travelling in a fifth-wheel trailer, yet you slapped on your oddball cap, and climbed up into the truck like an old hand. I was the anxious one, suffering in silence over how this was all going to work out. You were signalling that everything was going to be OK.

Meanwhile, I was becoming re-educated with Parkinson's Disease. It had been thirty years since I'd cared for Dad, and now I was witnessing a replay of all the familiar symptoms—the expressionless facial mask, the hand tremors, the shuffling gait, and legs that simply locked up at inconvenient times. Remember when you explained that if you turned (pivoted) too quickly, you'd fall over? And your smart aleck sister was quick to reply, "Well, that's easy to remedy, turn slowly?" The trouble with that sage advice was that you could never remember to do that. And so you regularly pivoted in haste and fell. And I'd ball you out. I'm still amazed how often you fell without breaking something.

I'll never forget the day we arrived at the Canadian border, holding our breath that the proceedings would go smoothly. Dick parked the trailer, and went ahead to the Customs Office with your documents to start the ball rolling. I was praying they wouldn't feel compelled to search the entire trailer or we'd be there until Christmas. Meanwhile, you were dealing with such a major case of the nerves over the impending border confrontation, you could scarcely walk. "Don't worry," I said, calmly. "Dick's looking after everything inside. We'll just take it slow and easy." You finally got your feet unlocked, and we began the trek from the truck to the Customs Office. We had everything under control, until you unexpectedly whirled around to check whether I'd locked the trailer. In the blink of an eye you were sprawled across the tarmac. "Not again," I admonished. "You know turning like that makes you fall!" You bounced back to your feet with surprising ease, brushed yourself off, and said, "I staged that so Customs will feel sorry for me." (The King black humour surfaces again!) I assured you that every customs officer in the place would have witnessed your performance on centre stage, the question is whether it would influence their handling of your case. Blessedly, they settled for your signature on a couple of documents, and waved us on our way. Whew! Home sweet home.

We pulled up to our home on a sunny warm day in mid-October. I offered you the choice of the upstairs bedroom with your own bathroom, or the equivalent downstairs. You were quick to choose the more private downstairs, claiming you have no difficulty with stairs. And you certainly knew. When we'd go for a walk together, your legs would lock up at any given moment, but our basement stairs? You popped up and down them like a teenager.

Once you had settled in, and the welcome party of nieces and nephews had come and gone, we went to work on the pesky pile of application forms confronting us. You needed a Social Insurance Number, an Alberta Health card, Blue Cross membership, a senior transit pass, photo ID, and a bank account. Plus, we needed to find you a doctor, a dentist, and a place to live. We accomplished all but the last item in the first week. Weren't we a team? When we got to the issue of living arrangements, it was the first time we weren't on the same page.

You were wanting to maintain your independence in a place of your own, but I was firm that you needed a setting that provided meals and the capability to oversee your welfare. Your resistance to senior residences was one I've heard before—"There's only old people in there." Once I won you over, we had a good time making the rounds in search of the right place.

Boardwalk Retirement Centre, just a six-minute run from our home, was the fourth place we visited. We both responded to its *feel* the moment we stepped through its front door. The smiling residents greeting us gave it such warmth. As we nodded in agreement, something interesting happened. Call it providence. Boardwalk Retirement Centre occupied one of two sixteen-floor buildings on shared property. Its twin was rented to the general public. We came calling just as the demand for senior care was mushrooming. To meet the need, management was beginning to convert its general apartments, as they became available, into senior independent living accommodation. The drawback for the seniors living in the secondary building was having to walk outside to the other building for meals—difficult for those with mobility issues, and inconvenient in inclement weather. You were overjoyed with the arrangement. You could eat with the old people, but live with the young people. Then fate delivered something even better—the first converted apartment to become available was on the sixteenth floor—the penthouse! Moving day was New Year's Day, 2015.

It was brutally cold, but you shrugged it off as if it was an everyday occurrence for you—as if you'd lived here all along. I have a sinking feeling that I never told you how impressed I was with your brave resolve to step forth into your new world, without complaint. So I'm telling you now. You never displayed a hint of *poor me*. Boardwalk was now your home, and the surrounding people—old and young—were your new family. This was your life now.

Your first act of the day was to dig out your Hudson Bay blanket coat to manage winter's wrath. Good grief, you wore that in high school. I tried to picture how many years and miles it had travelled with you, wilting in the back of the closet in LA, awaiting its final move back home. Once again, you were the Canuck in the red coat. My gang—husband, son, daughter, and two strapping grandsons—delivered furniture and boxes as fast as the elevator could haul them up sixteen floors. You put on your stage manager hat, and issued directions as they came through the door. We had everything in place by suppertime. The gang left for some well-earned take-out pizzas, and you and I washed up and headed for the dining room in the *old person* building. It had turned dark by then. Remember how we both turned—slowly, slowly—in the doorway, to look back at our day's work—your cozy sitting room, softly bathed in the glow of your Tiffany lamp, which you had strategically placed in the window? We had every reason to smile.

You settled in quickly, the many familiar items surrounding you, making your apartment truly yours. You concealed my old metal typing table with an Egyptian tapestry from Dad's restaurant, and dressed it up with Boston and New York mementos. I stitched the matching tapestry onto a rod, which we hung in the sitting area, already highlighted with Mother's brocade antique chair. I was a little surprised when you asked if I still had the old school map of Canada that you'd retrieved from our high school when it was closing down years before. Of course I had it, stashed in a corner of our basement. So I dug it out, and you featured it on your bedroom wall. What's with that? The guy who hated school, waking up every morning to a giant reminder of school smacking him in the face? Mother's antique dresser graced another wall—it had circulated through family members since I first left home. Now it shared your bedroom with a map. Were you ready for the bedspread? The one that Mother had made for your room when we were in high school? You had insisted on choosing the fabric yourself— large green checks in a sort of hemp-like fabric. I hope you still liked it, because it was back on your bed after living in our cabin for thirty years. In the weeks to follow, you came up with a few surprises of your own.

I'll never forget the day I dropped in for a visit, to discover a lovely triple-panelled room divider with walnut-coloured wooden slats, tastefully placed between your sitting area and the kitchenette. "Where did you get that beauty?" I asked. "Oh, I picked it up on sale at London Drug," you said, casually. By this time a neighbour in your residence had shown you a shortcut route to London Drug, and you were walking there with your cane most days. "Yes, but they don't deliver, do they?" I asked. "No, they don't, and the clerk was concerned about me managing, but I told her not to worry. I wrestled it out the door on my own." "And then what was your plan?" I asked. "Well, I'm not really sure, but it all worked out. A guy came along in a truck, and rolled down his window, 'Do you need any help, sir?' So I said yes, and he popped the divider into his truck box, and, well, here it is." I could only smile.

How many days later did I arrive to discover a coat rack parked beside the divider? Its walnut colour was a perfect match, and hanging from each coiled tentacle was a cap from your collection, everything from your out-of-character baseball cap, to the classy tweed driving cap that I brought you from *Lingards* in Preston, to your purple and gold high school beanie. "When did this arrive?" I asked. "Just yesterday," you said, grinning smugly. "I got it at London Drug."

"And did some guy come along in a truck?" I asked. "Well, as a matter of fact … " One final apartment item, a small shelf unit that held your telephone and what-nots, turned up one day, finding a perfect spot beside the kitchen table. I just smiled and said, "That's the perfect piece for that spot!" I didn't ask how it got there. You knew that Dick was always more than willing to help you, but I knew that you wanted to maintain as much independence as you could. And that's what you did.

I'll be honest, once you had your apartment decorated to your liking, I pictured you spending most of your time cocooned in it, with the exception of meals—sort of eat and retreat. But you surprised me. The guy who didn't want to live with a bunch of old people, became fully engaged in their world. Instrumental in welcoming you into the fold was Betty, the grandmother of my daughter-in-law, Michelle, who had lived in Boardwalk for a number of years. Betty volunteered daily, organizing the library, directing a choir, or rolling scrumptious baking out of her little kitchen for special occasions. Betty played piano and organ, and had a beautiful singing voice. You could also sing, but claimed that your Parkinson's stole your voice. "Linda Ronstadt has Parkinson's Disease," you said, "and she can't sing anymore." "But you're not Linda Ronstadt," I argued. "Have you even tried to sing? Why don't you give it a shot." So you did, and before you knew it you were in Betty's choir. And she was so happy to have you. Better still, you and Betty became fast friends.

You picked up a pool cue for the first time since we were kids shooting pool in our rumpus room, and even entered tournaments. Once you even won a tournament when your opponent accidentally sank the eight ball. You didn't care how the victory came about, or the fact that you hadn't sunk a single ball. Betty joined you for a game once, but it did not go well. Rounding the table to set up for her next shot, she snagged the edge of her shoe on the carpet, fell, and broke her pelvis. The intern in Emergency asked her how she fell. "I was playing pool," she said. "How can you fall in a pool?" he asked. "No, I wasn't *in* a pool," she explained. "I was *shooting* pool. You know, billiards." The intern couldn't wait to tell fellow interns about his ninety-three-year-old female patient who shoots pool.

Your residence held a fifty-fifty raffle every week as a fundraiser, and you volunteered to run it. You had an ulterior motive—it was a good way to get to know the names of your fellow residents. Soon you were calling them all by name, and they all knew your name. Friday night was movie night, and you noted that attendance was poor. The residents were weary of repeated, dull documentaries chosen by the man in charge, and he in turn was tiring of his Friday night responsibility. I suggested we could find some great movies at the library, and you could offer an intro before every screening—a story about one of the actors, the director, the screenplay. It was right up your alley. I didn't have to make the suggestion twice. Off we went to the library, got you a card, and after your first Friday, you were presenting to a packed house. I still laugh when I remember the day that I arrived at your apartment to find you sorting through a giant bag of old classics, clearly not issued by the library. "I found a five-for-a-buck bin in the mall," you said, grinning with pride. You had dragged home all you could carry.

I'm sure you'd agree that your two years at Boardwalk were positive years for you. Daily, you encountered the goodness in people. Greg, the manager of the complex, became a supportive friend, fellow residents embraced you warmly, and total strangers—some driving trucks—came to your rescue. Your medical needs were looked after by kind and skilled doctors—your primary caregiver, the neurologist and the psychiatrist at the mobility clinic, and the dermatologist, who gave you the same attention he'd give to someone half your age in the peak of health. I remember him conscientiously removing basal cell carcinomas and arranging for home care to change your dressings, as though you were going to live forever. Tuesdays were special, the day you had a standing date with our Diane—coffee and pie at Harvey's.

Your stories of Calgary's good people coming to your aid used to bring tears to my eyes. Twice you found yourself in trouble crossing the Charleswood Drive overpass returning to your building from a shopping excursion to London Drug or Safeway. Both times you were caught in severe wind, heavily laden with your purchases. You certainly didn't shy from a challenge, did you? Well, one time, a pedestrian came along, scooped up your bags, and offered you his arm. It turned out he lived in the same complex as you, so he delivered you and your parcels right to your door! The other time, a woman driver spotted you clinging to the railing of the overpass, fighting for survival against hurricane-like winds. She parked her car, leapt out, and grabbed your bags. "Take my arm, sir," she said. "I'll drive you home." Aware that traffic was already building behind her car, you resisted, saying, "Thank you, but, look, you're holding up a lot of cars." "Never mind them," she said. "They can just wait. Come, I'm driving you home." She had established her priority—hang the rest of the world. Bless her.

The story you told of your foray downtown on a winter day brought tears to your eyes, as well as mine, when you related it to me. We had previously gone downtown on the LRT together as a practice run, and this day you were taking it on solo. You felt like a change of scenery, and you always loved our downtown. But you picked a day that even your Hudson Bay blanket coat was hard-pressed to cope with. It was bitterly cold, the streets were slippery, and a high wind was making your walkabout near impossible. Once again you were clinging to a lamppost, wondering how you were going to get back home, when a young man stepped up and offered his arm. "Sir, take my arm. Where are you going?" "I guess I better get back to the LRT station," you said, "but I doubt that's where you're going." "It's where I'm going now," he said, without hesitation. The two-block walk gave you time to ask the young man about himself. He offered that he had just been released from jail three days prior, and he was feeling a little anxious about life on the outside. The best you could offer under the circumstances was your conviction that he was going to find his way, that he had all the qualities to succeed in life. Suddenly the train was there, and he saw you safely onboard, before turning to leave. You thanked him, and waved goodbye out the window as the train pulled away. You never forgot his friendly wave back.

The story you loved telling the most centred around the little five-year-old boy who lived in your building. Mario was a fetching little Asian boy who reminded you of yourself at that age—outgoing, bold, and ever ready to strike up a conversation with an adult. You enjoyed your chats with Mario whenever you met in the hall or on the elevator. By coincidence, you went through one lengthy stretch where you did not encounter one another. You had begun to wonder whether his family had moved. Then one day, you stepped off the elevator, and there was Mario in the lobby with his mother. "Oh yay! there you are," he shouted, running toward you. "I thought you were dead!"

Well, Don, you and I had two good years together, didn't we—lunch in old Central Park (now Central Memorial

Park), where our parents courted; evenings at Theatre Calgary, which impressed your critical eye; nostalgic walks through the neighbourhood of our youth; strolls through the downtown, bemoaning the absence of old landmarks; drives through a city you scarcely recognized; and trips to the mountains that you knew and loved. Every excursion concluded with an ice cream cone, at your insistence. Guess what happened when I was sifting through your files one day? A news clipping fell from a folder, and floated to the floor. I picked it up, and burst out laughing when I read, "Advice for seniors troubled with weight loss: eat some ice cream every day." Thanks a lot, Mr. 110-pounder! Not my problem.

The changes as your Parkinson's progressed were subtle … until they weren't. You began falling more frequently, and your anxiety level rose. You resisted turning in your cane for a walker, until Greg, the Boardwalk manager, insisted. Then you admitted that you really did need the stability the walker offered. Remember the day we were a full half hour late for your psychiatrist appointment because your legs repeatedly locked up on the walk from the parkade to his office? But you didn't like the idea of my dropping you off at the office building—you liked the security of having me by your side. I get that. So we soldiered on. And we found tolerant, kind people everywhere. I remember taxi and bus drivers waiting ever so patiently behind the crosswalk leading to your doctor's office, while your balking legs took forever to navigate the road. People witnessing the scene were unsure how to help, but that didn't stop them from running to us with offers nevertheless. Only once I remember encountering a woman on an elevator who had no patience as you struggled to step in. Granted, she did not have the benefit of knowing that you had Parkinson's, or that difficulty *crossing a threshold* is a common problem for Parkinson sufferers. But I'm not sure it would have made a difference in any event. I can still see her angry glare as she barked at me, "That man needs to be in a wheelchair. Why don't you get him one?" She talked over you as though you didn't exist, and addressed me like I was too stupid to have a clue what you needed. I haven't forgotten the collective gasp from the others on the elevator who knew better.

As your disease progressed further, you developed difficulty swallowing, which led to aspiration pneumonia. I began bracing for the end. You were hospitalized twice and treated with oxygen. Both times you were discharged in a weakened state, and looking generally unwell. My heart sank when Diane, who loved her standing dates with you for pie and coffee, called in distress one Tuesday: "Mom, Uncle Don fell over and over again when we went for pie today, even using his walker. I lost count how many times I picked him up." That was your last pie date together. A week later, Dick and I took you on an outing to shop for a few needs. We delivered you home in time for your supper, and I kissed you goodbye. I had no idea that it was our last date together.

You had supper with your Boardwalk family, then enjoyed a heartwarming evening with Nora, another musically gifted friend. The two of you decided to play a DVD of Broadway songs, and since you both knew all the lyrics, you had a singalong together. Then you went off to your apartment and called me. You were anxious about managing newly prescribed strategies to aid with swallowing. I urged you to try to set your concerns aside, said that I'd be calling in the morning, and we'd take on the new day together. "It's time for your warm shower now," I said, "and a good night's sleep." You had a fatal heart attack in the shower. We had no new day together. I thought I was ready for this, but I wasn't.

Before I wind this up, I thought you might like to know what happened next. You certainly left your mark on Boardwalk. Gregory confessed that he'd become inured to death in all his years of confronting it so routinely, but losing you caught him off guard. He was in full mourning over you. Nora was beside herself. She had so enjoyed your singsong the night before, she was devastated that you were gone. Betty was not just losing a member of her choir, but a dear friend. Many others phoned to express what you meant to them, and how much you would be missed. And so, even though you had always specified you wanted no service, I could see that I had to do something for your Boardwalk family. The choice was easy, I'd do the Friday night movie. I knew that you had wanted to show your all-time favourite, *Sunset Boulevard*, but it was a title that had eluded us at the library. Nothing eludes Diane. She ordered a rush copy online, and it arrived in time for Friday.

Dick, Diane, and Stephen joined me for the event, and instead of paying homage to Gloria Swanson as a preamble, I offered a history of your theatrical beginnings … in Aunt Lil's basement when you were twelve. Remember how the neighbours flocked to plays that you wrote and directed? And how Aunt Lil had to scramble for chairs? Well, you're still packing them in. Now Dick and the kids were scrambling for chairs to accommodate the Boardwalk crowd. I also remember you getting irritated when the same attendees habitually walked out of your Friday night movie midway through, because it was past their bedtime. Not this Friday. Every last one stayed up long after the movie ended to share stories of you, their friend. One woman jumped to her feet, and, breathless with excitement, said she was going to approach Boardwalk about naming its modest, makeshift theatre the Don King Theatre. I highly doubted that her idea would come to fruition, but I was touched by her thought. To close the evening, I sent them all to bed with a printed copy of your obituary, which I found on your computer. (We should all have the good sense to write our own obituaries—who knows our own history better than we ourselves?) Here's a replay to refresh your memory:

> *King, Donald Emerson, beloved brother of Dr. Stanley King of Ottawa and Eleanor King Byers of Calgary, died in Calgary on November 10, 2016 at the age of 82 years. Born April 4, 1934 in Calgary, he was the son of the late Horace King, well known Calgary restaurateur and Ruby Loan Hall King (nee Anderson). He was predeceased by a nephew, Douglas Byers. Both Donald and his father had Parkinson's Disease. He attended Connaught and Sunalta public schools and Central High School. He was a former member of Wesley United Church and Scarboro United Church.*
>
> *His growing up years in Calgary were chronicled in his sister's memoir, The House With The Light On, published in 2003. In addition to his brother and sister, he is survived by his sister-in-law, Mina King of Ottawa, his brother-in-law, Richard Byers of Calgary, two nieces, Diane Howell of Calgary and Jennifer King of Ottawa, two nephews, Stephen Byers of Calgary and David King of Ottawa, two great-nieces, two great nephews, and five cousins. Don briefly attended Gonzaga University in Spokane, Washington before transferring to the University of British Columbia where he received a B.A. degree in English and psychology. He was a member of the Beta Theta Pi fraternity at U.B.C.*

Following graduation, he appeared in Vancouver Little Theatre productions, and was an assistant stage manager with Theatre Under The Stars in Stanley Park.

Following five years in Vancouver, Don was accepted at Boston University's Graduate School of Theatre. He earned his tuition as a room service waiter in a hotel near the campus. He appeared in lead roles in major productions with fellow student Faye Dunaway while earning a master's degree in fine arts. His hometown newspaper, The Calgary Herald, reported that among Boston's 2,000 graduates in 1962, Donald King was the only Calgarian. His graduate thesis performance as Charles, the Dauphin, in the North American premiere of the Christopher Fry translation of The Lark by Jean Anouilh, received glowing reviews. Following graduation, he moved to New York where his first job was assistant to the maître d' and stage manager of the Plaza Hotel's celebrated nightclub, the Persian Room. While working with stars such as Robert Goulet, Ethel Merman, Liza Minelli, and Juliet Prowse, he accepted an invitation to guest lecture at the University of Minnesota's drama department. From there he returned to New York where he spent the next ten years stage managing Broadway and off-Broadway productions, fashion shows, regional theatre, and summer stock. A highlight was stage managing Julius Monk's cabaret revue in it last season at the Plaza Hotel.

He then moved to Los Angeles where, in addition to stage managing, he taught speech to aspiring actors and tried his hand at writing for television. His first produced story, for Norman Lear's sitcom Maude, *starring Bea Arthur, was nominated for a Humanitas Prize. Don was a staff writer on* Mamma's Family, *a dialogue director on* A New Kind of Family, *and worked with producers developing projects for television, including the southern classic novel,* Thorpe, *with Lucy Antek Johnson, who later became CBS Vice-President of daytime programming. After living away from his hometown for fifty years, he returned to his roots in 2014. At Don's request, there will be no service. Following cremation his remains will be placed next to his parents in Union Cemetery.*

For many years, you had been working on two writing projects in LA—one, a lengthy article of your Persian Room experiences entitled *Persian Nights,* ambitiously targeted for the *New Yorker* magazine, and the other. a book that changed titles as it progressed. It began life as *The Pecking Order*, down the road became *A Bigot's Guide to Prejudice*, and by the time it hit Calgary it had adopted the facetious title, *No Rich Man Is Ugly*. You'd had your manuscripts professionally edited to prepare them for submitting, and I computerized them. Alas, we never landed a publisher, did we? I would have persisted after you were gone, except I came to the regrettable conclusion that both these stories had passed their *best before* dates.

As you would expect, I found a home for your clothes and personal effects, and then I started through your *real* treasures, your written material. Boxes and boxes of it. We writers don't know how to part with paper, do we? My first task was to sift through your personal correspondence with the intent to inform your friends of your passing. I discovered that you collected friends at each stop in your journey—Spokane, Vancouver, Boston, New York, LA—and corresponded with them forever after. Now it was my turn. I found email addresses for Lucy and Barbara—addresses they sent you in hopes that you'd write them electronically. But technology was never your long suit, so you never did. But I did. And all the others, I wrote in the old-fashioned way.

I don't need to remind you what beautiful friends you have. Most responded with warm, thoughtful stories of their times with you. From San Juan, Myrna wrote of her Boston University days with you, when she cooked Puerto Rican food for the gang in her tiny apartment, and you all talked endlessly about the theatre. Judy, another Boston alum, wrote, "Thanks for sharing this 'Last Act' of Don's life with me. I will miss him." Bud was heartbroken. You and he dated back to summer stock at the Falmouth Playhouse when you were rookies. Ruth wrote at length from England, "Don and I worked together for two and a half years in New York, and then we wrote for fifty years after that." Dottie wrote that you and she had rented suites in the same brownstone in New York fifty years prior. Her heartwarming letter came in a large padded envelope accompanied by two copies of her favourite book, *The Velveteen Rabbit*, and a packet of old Christmas cards that you'd sent her. Virgil wrote six pages in his ornamental, oversized cursive, filling me in on your Boston days together, your current mutual friends, and topics that you and he communicated through the years—your respective projects, the Royal family, the state of politics in the US. His letter also included a whole packet of your cards and letters sent to him, dating back to the '60s. He, like you, had moved back to his hometown at the urging of his family. "Hectic and fraught days," he described his move, "but I got my belongings down to one covered wagon ... though piled high." Virgil is a character.

But wait till you hear this! Ruth and Dottie and Virgil all adopted me full on. Penpals! Dottie has sent whole care packages containing books she's "wanting to find a good home for," news clips about Canada, Peanuts cartoons, and for our granddaughters Lindsay and Kalyn, photos, picture books and fancy bookmarks she "thinks they may like." And stuffed into a recent parcel: "Look what I found! More cards and letters from Don!" I burst into tears the day I received a letter from Dottie's lawyer, informing me of her death. (The lawyer found me in Dottie's box of letters.) Your dear friend, and *mine*, is gone. Ruth and Virgil continue to write.

By now you must be thinking that this letter is never going to end, but there's one last thing that I wish we'd talked about a bit more—your declaration of being an atheist. You confessed to me that you were unsure of it yourself, until the day you heard a man on TV expounding on his life theories, and they all aligned with yours. When he announced his atheism at the conclusion of his talk, your overriding thought was, "Aha, that's what I must be!" Even so, I never believed that you strayed entirely from our Christian upbringing. You left too much evidence.

In your autobiographical obituary, you named the churches that our family had attended. Granted, you specified being a *former* member, but the fact remains, you chose to include them in your life story. Secondly, after your trip to England with Lucy, you were positively breathless recounting the "most memorable Christmas Eve of [your] life." You had attended the heart-stopping service in St. Paul's Cathedral where you were overwhelmed with the cathedral's magnificence and the beauty of its centrepiece—the crèche. And lastly, I have your Bible, which I found in your book collection. It's an interesting edition: the *King James Version* we grew up with, but "designed to be read as living literature," which makes it much more readable. I'm wondering if it was perhaps part of your studies somewhere along the line? In any event, underlined passages and comments pencilled into margins all over the place tell me that you had read it from cover to cover. All 1,230 pages.

Finally, we had a conversation nearing the end of your days that left a hollow feeling in the pit of my stomach. You said to me, "I don't know why people talk about an afterlife. When you die, there's nothing." Then you threw up your arms and upped the volume to emphasize the point—"NOTHING!" When I came to your apartment the morning you died, you were still on the floor where the Boardwalk caregivers had found you. I knelt down, gave you a goodbye kiss, and whispered in your ear, "So, tell me, is there nothing?" You didn't answer, so I guess I'll have to wait to find out for myself. But one thing I do know, there are a lot of people here who think about you every day and continue to love you. And that's not nothing.

Well, my brother, I've carried on, haven't I? But I think I have gotten to know you a little better than when I began this letter, days and pages ago. If you're still with me, I'll wrap it up with words from Ellen Goodman, your all-time favourite journalist. Remember how you used to rave about Ellen, and regularly sent me clippings of her columns? So I think it's fitting that I bring this to a close with a quote from a piece of hers, entitled, *Treasure or Trash?* My turn to clip this time. I found this piece of hers in the April 15, 2002, issue of the *National Post*. With her renowned humour, Ellen described her challenge, as a self-confessed packrat, to deal with the annual dreaded rite of spring cleaning. Wrestling with what's important to keep and what to let go, she boiled it down to "dividing history from clutter." Her conclusion gives me assurance that all these boxes of paper that you and I can't part with are not clutter, they're history. Without them, how would the generations to follow ever get to know us?

> *"What the next generation will value most is not what we owned, but the evidence of who we were and the tales of how we loved. In the end, it's the family stories that are worth the storage."*
>
> Ellen Goodman.

Love you!
Your big sis, El

—Afterword—

How many of us have been annoyed with ourselves for neglecting to ask questions of our parents until it was too late? Why didn't I ask Dad more about … ? Darn, I should've asked Mother why … ? Let me remind you, it's not entirely too late. As I wrote to my family members who'd gone ahead, I made a surprising discovery: the mere act of putting down those unasked questions on paper, magically produced some answers. I know my parents and my brother a little better now. I understand what made them tick, and the misfortunes that stood in the way of them ticking at their full potential. I have felt the weight of their burdens as never before. Hopefully, I've lightened them a bit.

Getting to know my four grandparents has been the journey of a lifetime. They were the impetus for this pilgrimage at the outset, and look where it brought us! I began my story with the supposition that family traits typically skip a generation. Since I had no grandparents in my life, I began my journey to validate this theory in a void. Here's what I have pieced together:

I acquired my love of sewing from both my grandmothers. I hope they might even offer their stamp of approval for some of my achievements, even though I confess that I'm a slave to commercial patterns. I know they both pretty much winged their projects. Grandma King designed and stitched costumes specifically for Grandpa's theatrical productions, and Grandmother Anderson produced whole wardrobes for her girls using any available source, including pieces scrounged from their father's old suits and her own frayed-at-the-cuff dresses. Her little girls were so beautifully turned out, they had no idea they were poor. Beyond the sewing machine, I sense that I'd have little in common with Grandmother Anderson. Staid and proper, she was geared to girls and feminine things. My life has been overrun with boys who didn't have much use for proper. Family members all said Grandmother Anderson possessed a regal bearing. The closest I ever got to regal was my King name. I sort of imagine I'd be more comfortable with Grandma King, who would have been hard-pressed to maintain order—with regal bearing or otherwise—in her household of rowdies, ruled by the restless, hyperactive man of the house. I'm not sure if I possess the confidence she must have mustered to launch a successful antique business, but I don't dismiss the prospect.

Now, my grandfathers: I unquestionably share Grandpa King's love for music and live theatre, but the thought of actually performing solo on stage is unthinkable, even if I had the talent. Which I don't. Brother Don got both his own share and mine. I picture Grandpa King as a take-charge extrovert who bored through life in high gear, waiting for no man who couldn't keep up. In stark contrast, I view Grandpa Anderson as a guy taking life at a calm, easy pace, one day at a time. I am mindful, of course, that his life-altering encounter with tuberculosis may have factored in his demeanour.

In the end, my strongest kinship is with Grandpa Anderson, probably for two main reasons. The first, I sense that his easy-going personality, whether impacted by his tuberculosis or not, would have most closely aligned with mine. Secondly, I simply know him the best, thanks to my mother and my brother Stan keeping him alive for me with their stories. Mother talked about him often—her fun-loving father who counterbalanced her serious, strait-laced mother. How often did I hear her repeat his sayings, which my family now catches me repeating?: "July 12 is the hottest day of the year in Calgary."—not up for debate; "It's only money."—when Mother laughingly said he didn't have any; "There's all the time there is."—when he'd run out of that, too; "I'll do it *the day after tomorrow."*— a moving target.

It's been a joy getting to know all these beautiful people. Every letter I wrote deepened my love for each of them. The most noteworthy conclusion I have made is this: although individual personalities of my family members varied widely, they had much in common when it came to qualities that count the most—devotion to family, adherence to honesty and decency, and commitment to an unshakeable moral code. I am blessed that they are mine.

Acknowledgements

Grateful thanks to the talented FriesenPress team, who walked me through the publishing process with careful attention to every detail. With an honourable mention to Kate, who patiently took me by the hand each step of the way.

To my six beautiful King cousins, holding them in my heart while writing to the members of our family, has buoyed me continuously:

The children of Dad's brother Walter, who have all gone ahead—Ethel, our trusted matriarch who led the way; Art, the family jokester, who led us in laughter the whole way; and Frank, whose Olympic dream showed the world Calgary's way. They are loved and missed. I will write to them next. Special thanks to Jeanette, Frank's widow, whose continued kinship I cherish, for surprising me with invaluable King family treasures and photos, discovered amongst Frank's effects.

My *double* cousins—children of Dad's brother, Harry, and Mother's sister, Lillian—Marion, the family achiever, who succeeded at everything; Rich, my contemporary and partner in crime growing up; and Audrey, the baby of the family, who arrived too late to experience some of our goings on, but has since made it her mission to know the family better than any of us. A special shout-out to Audrey, for her readiness to share her collection of family information, memorabilia, and one-of-a-kind photos.

To my lone Anderson cousin, Nick—actually my *double second* cousin—gratitude for recording and sharing his wealth of Anderson family stories. (You're asking, is there such a thing as a *double second* cousin? Yes, it's easy—Nick is the son of my mother's *double first* cousin.) We only found Nick as adults—or rather, he found us, while researching his family tree.

To big brother, Stan—the lucky one in my immediate family, having had a grandpa in his everyday world for his first eight years—I am thankful for his willingness to consider the endless questions I pose, even though he frequently draws a blank, when the assignment is to fill in the blanks. Sometimes, however, when we combine our two half-memories, we come up with a whole story. Yay! And I'm the lucky one, having had this special guy in my world for all of my years.

Lastly, to my husband, Dick, who had the good fortune to marry into the best family in the world—at least that's what I've been telling him for the past sixty-three years—my gratitude for all the loving care he's showered upon us ... as though he agreed with me. I am grateful for his devotion, and his patience during all those days when I was holed up in my office writing letters.

Printed in the USA
CPSIA information can be obtained
at www.ICGtesting.com
JSHW011412251123
52351JS00004B/9